T'

13.0

12.10

19.1

14.

22.

OR 6/93

Country Textiles of Japan

COUNTRY TEXTILES OF JAPAN

The Art of Tsutsugaki

by Reiko Mochinaga Brandon

New York • WEATHERHILL • *Tokyo*

This book has been published to coincide with an exhibition organized by the author under the sponsorship of
the Honolulu Academy of Arts and first held at the
Academy from May 22 through June 29, 1986.

First edition, 1986

Published by John Weatherhill, Inc., New York and
Tokyo, with editorial offices at 7-6-13 Roppongi,
Minato-ku, Tokyo 106, Japan. Protected by copyright
under terms of the International Copyright Union; all
rights reserved.   Printed in Japan.

Library of Congress Cataloging in Publication Data: Brandon,
Reiko Mochinaga. / Country textiles of Japan. / Bibli-
ography: p. / Includes index. / 1. Resist-dyed textiles—
Japan—Technique. 2. Textile fabrics—Japan—History—
Edo period, 1600–1868. / I. Honolulu Academy of Arts.
II. Title. / NK9504.7.B7   1986   746.6′6   86-5591 /
ISBN 0-8348-0207-4

FOR JIM

Contents

Country Textiles of Japan

Introduction

Tsutsugaki, literally "tube drawing," is a Japanese term that describes a widely used resist-dyeing technique. Thick rice paste is squeezed through the tip of a cone-shaped tube (*tsutsu*) onto the surface of a flat cloth. The artisan draws (*kaki* or *gaki*) free-hand patterns with the paste that he wishes to remain uncolored when dyes or pigments are applied to the cloth. While the uncovered fabric absorbs the color, the hardened rice paste prevents coloring agents from reaching the covered patterned areas—hence the name "paste resist" for this technique. The thick, adhesive paste dries into a solid mass that totally resists dye penetration and even after repeated immersions retains a firm edge. As a result, in textiles created by the tsutsugaki method, sharply defined white lines and clear-cut patterns typically stand out against a dyed background.

During the Edo period (1603–1868), Japanese textile craftsmen created many types of fabrics using the freehand, paste-resist tsutsugaki technique. Two of the most highly prized are *chayazome,* an elegant summer cloth made of ramie and worn exclusively by women of the upper samurai class, and *yūzen,* a celebrated dyed silk produced in Kyoto which only the most wealthy could afford. These expensive fabrics were created by skilled urban artisans who followed every whim of fashion in the attempt to please their stylish patrons. Although chayazome and yūzen employ tsutsugaki techniques, they are not usually called tsutsugaki textiles.

The term tsutsugaki, as a textile description, is reserved for those utilitarian fabrics made of cotton and hemp that were created by the tsutsugaki technique for commoners. Tsutsugaki textiles for the common people were made both in cities and in the countryside. Everywhere the general techniques were the same and ideas from one area easily carried into another. Most Japanese experts do not distinguish between urban and country tsutsugaki, and indeed such ordinary textiles as curtains (*noren*), wrapping cloths (*furoshiki*), and banners (*nobori*) were common in city and country alike. Nonetheless, to some extent people in towns lived differently from their cousins in the country and hence the types of textiles they considered essential or desirable differed to some extent as well. Tsutsugaki artisans in the great cities of Edo and Osaka developed special skill and fluency in making the bold-patterned coats worn by firemen (*hikeshi hanten*), shop clerks' work uniforms (*hanten*), and banners used for outdoor advertising or display. These textiles, while also made in the country, were in particular demand in commercial, urban centers. At the same time country tsutsugaki craftsmen, serving village communities where textiles held a special place, created unique ceremonial tsutsugaki designed to celebrate auspicious occasions: bridal bed covers (*futonji* and *yogi*), chest covers (*yutan*), ceremonial wrapping cloths, fishermen's ceremonial kimono (*maiwai*), baby towels (*yuage*), baby-carrying sashes (*kooi*), diapers (*mutsuki*), and special Boy's Day banners. A number of these textiles were wholly unique to the countryside; all of them were developed as a part of a textile tradition that was nourished in Japanese villages over many centuries.

Here the focus is on the work of the anonymous tsutsugaki craftsmen who worked in the little-known country tsutsugaki tradition. The present volume attempts to explore the aesthetic values and social usage of these visually beautiful, yet always utilitarian cotton fabrics. Many of the pieces chosen were created for the important rites of marriage and birth. Fortunately a significant number of fine ceremonial textiles made by village craftsmen during the late Edo and Meiji periods (19th and early 20th centuries) have survived. The majority of the examples gathered here have been drawn from the Textile Collection of the Honolulu Academy of Arts. A few have been lent by museums in Japan or are from private collections in Honolulu.

The many stunning works in the following pages witness the extraordinary skill of unnamed country craftsmen. They mirror the happiness and pride of their original owners, modest people who lived during the period of transition from feudal to modern Japan.

A simple outfit woven of natural fiber taken from wild mulberry bark covers a farmer tilling his fields in the rain. A curtain of homespun cotton dyed deeply in indigo blue demarks the entrance to a village merchant's shop. A padded winter sleeping kimono, decorated with felicitous crane and tortoise of rose and pale blue, protects a bride and groom against the bitter night's cold in a mountain hamlet.

Beautiful handmade textiles created out of humble materials clothed nine out of ten Japanese, decorated homes and shops, and answered people's aesthetic needs from distant times until less than a hundred years ago. Although country textiles are not as refined as the brocaded silk robes or elegantly embroidered kimono (*kosode*) produced by city artisans for Japan's samurai and imperial court, they possess both strength and beauty of their own. Japan's ruling and wealthy classes never made up more than seven percent of the population, yet because of their prestige and political power the textiles they used have been carefully preserved as family heirlooms or state treasures in temples, shrines, museums, and in private homes through the intervening centuries. Such treatment was never given to the woven garments and the textile furnishings of Japan's common people, however. Vast numbers of textiles that were made for this unknown majority perished in daily use, unseen and unsung beyond the villages in which they were made and used.

Recognition of Japan's ignored folk textile traditions belatedly began at the turn of this century, when anthropologists, philosophers, and artists first turned their attention to the study of village or folk culture. Foremost among them was the scholar and collector Yanagi Sōetsu (1889–1961), whose unique contribution was to establish for Japanese folk crafts their own aesthetic value. To Yanagi the beauty of folk craft was inseparable from function and arose from collective, anonymous labor. To describe folk arts—for which no word then existed in Japanese—Yanagi coined the term *mingei*: *min* from *minshu* (common people), *gei* from *kōgei* (crafts). In his profoundly insightful writings he championed an intuitive appreciation of folk crafts.

It was largely through Yanagi's work that the public was led to accept the hidden beauty of everyday, utilitarian artifacts. Yanagi argued that preservation of folk crafts was an important task, made urgent by the rapid mechanization of the country and subsequent decline in folk-craft production during the twentieth century. In 1936 he and his supporters established the Japan Folk Craft Museum (Nihon Mingeikan) in Tokyo and here a significant number of folk textiles have been preserved and exhibited. Two other important figures who contributed to the reassessment of traditional crafts were Yanagida Kunio (1875–1961) and Shibuzawa Keizō (1896–1963). Yanagida established the study of folklore (*minzoku*) as a scholarly subject in Japan. He traveled extensively in remote regions, studying folk customs and myths and the books he wrote about his discoveries remain landmarks of folklore scholarship. Shibuzawa, a wealthy financier and at one time minister of finance, was an avid collector of folk crafts who supported research and documentation of existing village crafts. Aesthetic qualities of crafts were emphasized in Yanagi's mingei approach; scholars in the minzoku movement promoted a functional, scientific view of crafts in society.

Today the Japanese public is sensitive to the value of folk art. Collection and research efforts go forward in a number of institutions and contemporary craftsmen find stimulus in working in the mingei tradition. The recognition of folk crafts came none too soon, for traditional crafts were on the verge of total disappearance in the early decades of this century. The efforts of Yanagi and others are especially noteworthy for the survival of country textiles, for without a reappraisal of the value of folk crafts, it is likely that far fewer examples of these objects of daily life would have survived for our appreciation today.

Throughout Japanese history textiles used by hard-working ordinary people have had a short life span. It is an interesting commentary on the intrinsic quality of country textiles that they were commonly recycled by their owners rather than put in storage or thrown away. A cotton farm kimono, for example, underwent a long journey of transformation from the time it was first worn to its final days as cloth scraps. The unique "straight-cut" construction of Japanese garments, in which front, back, and sleeves consist of rectangular pieces of cloth of the same width, made resewing and recycling easy. In the process of washing, sections would be rearranged to avoid further wear and badly worn sections would be discarded. In time, right and left sleeve panels were exchanged and resewn to replace frayed sleeve openings; long sleeves became shorter. An adult kimono would be transformed into a child's kimono or a sleeveless jacket and the sleeves resewn into square cushion covers. After a few more seasons, parts of the garment where the fiber was still strong would be made into baby's diapers. At the end of its journey, the kimono would be reduced to no more than kitchen rags. Or sometimes a village woman would painstakingly tear the worn kimono fabric into narrow strips and then reweave the strips into a new garment, a technique called *sakiori* (tear-and-weave). The recycling in the latter case was not merely recycling any more. Although the intention was practical, the result was a wholly new garment possessing a wonderful charm of its own. Textiles in villages were, indeed, utilized fully, leaving nothing to waste.

Country tsutsugaki textiles flourished in an environment of self-sufficiency. All the varied steps in the process of creating textiles for village use—collecting or growing fibers, spinning, weaving, dyeing, and needlework—could be and usually were carried out at home during breaks in farm and domestic chores, usually by women. "Durable," "inexpensive," and "locally obtainable" were the imperatives of their textile world. Materials and dyes came from the local environment. Wild fibers such as mulberry, Japanese linden, and wisteria could be gathered from the hillsides. Villagers cultivated hemp (*asa*)[1] and cotton in their own fields for their own use. Brown and grey dye sources for the familiar colors of country textiles were easily obtainable from the bark of local trees—chestnut, walnut, pasania, and oak. Phellodendron and miscanthus plants produced yellow dyes, another common color. Indigo plants, which produced the popular deep blue shades of country textiles, were originally cultivated by each village weaver-dyer for personal use. Even when specialization in growing, weaving, and dyeing developed in the countryside, the tradition of using local materials remained strong. Thus Japanese craft women and men created unique styles of textiles that arose from the special environment in which each lived.

Today local textile traditions survive in certain areas. For example, wild arrowroot (*kuzu*) fiber from which traditional raincoats used to be made is now woven into material for decorative sliding doors by people of Kakegawa in Shizuoka Prefecture. The coarse bark of Japanese linden (*shina*) provides fiber that inhabitants living in the mountains near Ikazuchi in Niigata Prefecture weave into sashes and curtains. Fiber from a species of wild banana (*ito bashō*) is the raw material of Okinawa's famous semi-transparent *bashōfu* textiles. The delicate crepe ramie (*chijimi*) of Ojiya in Niigata Prefecture achieves its pure white color and special texture by natural bleaching that occurs when the material is spread out on the deep snow of this cold region. Chestnut trees produce the celebrated earthy brown color seen in the striped cotton fabrics made in Tamba, Hyogo Prefecture. Compounds of iron naturally occur in muddy pools on Amami-Oshima Island; used as a mordant, the iron produces the deep black tone of Amami-Oshima ikat textiles. Folk textiles are the product of nature. They contain the textures, smells, and colors of the wild trees, leaves, and flowers that are woven and dyed into them.

Country textiles were made with simple tools and techniques. In most cases women wove on primitive looms, called *izaribata* (Figure 30). They were simple back-strap looms that did not have elaborate mechanical devices. As if to compensate for their rudimentary looms, which could not produce complicated designs or interesting patterns, villagers devoted long and tedious hours to pre- and post-weaving processes that accomplished the same aims. Checked and striped patterns were popular in the countryside because these patterns could easily be created in plain-weave structure by properly choosing threads that previously had been dyed the appropriate hues. The beautiful and complex patterns of Japanese *kasuri* (ikat) textiles are produced in many parts of Japan not by loom techniques but by laboriously tying and dyeing, often several times, bundles of warp and/or weft threads into predetermined patterns prior to weaving. Stitchery was another means of producing patterns on plain-woven cloth. With no more than needle and thread, women of the Tsugaru region of Aomori Prefecture produced the densely stitched work clothes known as *kogin*. Endless evening hours went into stitching diamonds, squares, triangles, lozenges, and other geometric patterns. Kogin material was exceptionally durable as well as prized for the attractiveness of its white-on-blue patterns.

Another common method of creating designs on plain-weave cloth was by dyeing the fabric after it was woven. Tsutsugaki dyeing required only the simplest tools, such as the cone that held the paste. As in weaving and stitching, tsutsugaki craftsmen were not dependent on mechanical devices to produce their creations. Rather success depended on the development of working skills through long patient hours spent on one's craft.

Under humble and self-sufficient circumstances, Yanagi points out, the artisan carried on his or her work as a normal, daily task. Out of this process an unassuming beauty quite naturally arises. More than anything else the modest beauty of tsutsugaki textiles shows what we might call "the quality of ease." It is an unconscious product born from the experienced hands of farm wives and village artisans who, year after year, earnestly made the same type of textiles. They did not work out of conscious artistic or aesthetic aspiration; nonetheless a sense of beauty unconsciously guided their hands. If their designs are simple and traditional, they are also assured and often possess spontaneous, powerful energy. Throughout their lives mothers and wives wove fabrics for husbands and children and village dyers dyed the cloth of neighbors and friends. If money was involved or pride, as it often was, the process of making textiles was a part of life as natural as eating and sleeping. Textiles gave comfort and pleasure. And beauty was inherent in the task of making them.

The exhibition pieces presented here are mainly celebratory cotton tsutsugaki (*tsutsugaki momen*), an important nineteenth-century manifestation of the tradition of country textiles. Celebratory cotton tsutsugaki are fundamentally utilitarian fabrics that were made for special, auspicious occasions. Often they were gifts. Because celebratory tsutsugaki textiles were valued by their owners, they were often stored away and little used, a fact which has contributed to their survival. Futonji, furoshiki, yutan, yuage, noren, and nobori were made from cloth woven by women in their homes, and dyed by specialist artisans living in small towns and villages in the countryside. The examples in the present work come mostly from the western Japan Sea coast (San'in), the north central coast (Hokuriku), northern Honshu (Tohoku), the island of Shikoku and the Inland Sea (Setonaikai), and Kyushu Island.

The precise origin of tsutsugaki textile technique is not known. Generally tsutsugaki is believed to have developed in China. The passage of tsutsugaki from China to Japan may have been direct or by way of Korea or the Ryukyu Islands (Okinawa). Kamakura Yoshitarō, artist-scholar, speculates that trading ships sailing between Taiwan, Okinawa, and Japan may have been the route for introducing tsutsugaki.[2] The famous *bingata* dyed cotton fabrics of Okinawa use tsutsugaki technique. In any case, drawing a paste-resist pattern onto fabric and then dyeing the fabric to produce designs of varied colors was being practiced in Japan by the mid-sixteenth century. Yūzen dyeing, which employed tsutsugaki technique, originated in Kyoto in the late seventeenth century. Kyoto yūzen artisans used a cone with an extremely small tip. With it they drew intricate motifs of fine lines on delicate silk fabrics. Dyes and pigments were carefully brushed onto the fabric and no dip-dyeing was involved. These specifics of the urban yūzen tradition are not a part of the basic country tradition of cotton tsutsugaki, but it seems probable that yūzen had an influence on the work of dyers of the countryside. The fundamental process of drawing with a cone is the same in both instances. We see in some country cotton bedding covers the same type of graduated shading (*bokashi*) that is so typical of yūzen fabrics. The drawn designs of some children's cotton ceremonial kimono made in the Meiji period (1868–1912) are close copies of typical yūzen motifs (the background of the cotton kimono, however, is dipped in pure blue indigo, which is not a yūzen technique). Thus, these cotton tsutsugaki textiles were sometimes disparagingly termed "country yūzen" (*inaka yūzen*).

The unusually strong visual impact of cotton tsutsugaki give them a special position among village textiles. The designs are dynamic and assured. Sometimes delightfully humorous images emerge from a dexterously wielded tsutsu. Each cotton tsutsugaki piece is unique, for even when the design is based on a well-known and traditional motif, it is spontaneously drawn freehand and no two designs can ever be drawn alike. In this respect the art of cotton tsutsugaki is energetic and free, and unique among other country weaving and dyeing traditions, such as kasuri or stencil-resist dyeing (*katazome*), which fundamentally repeat a fixed design. The vigorous, vivid images of cotton tsutsugaki seem to clearly convey the common people's deep feelings at times of celebration. The carefully crafted country tsutsugaki fabrics are strong statements about the goodness and the potential of life. They look to the future—of a new couple, a newly born child. In them, people's energy and emotion, usually suppressed in hard-working daily life, burst forth on special joyous occasions. Auspicious phoenix, lion, crane, and turtle fly, jump, and swim on garments, bedding, and banners. Even large family crests, originally denied to commoners, take their place in tsutsugaki design as an expression of common people's pride.

The energy and freedom reflected in these textiles are also a product of the particular time in which cotton tsutsugaki were produced. The late Edo period was a time of social and economic transition in Japan. The strict feudal system with the shogun ruling at the top of the Tokugawa hierarchy was finally coming to its end. For two centuries the merchant class had gradually accumulated tremendous wealth and, consequently, the status and financial power of the samurai class were eroded. The boundary between the four social classes—samurai, farmers, craftsmen, and merchants—was no longer, if it ever was, a barrier to advancement. Samurai tried to be merchants (usually unsuccessfully), merchants bought samurai status, farmers sold goods, and commercial centers were born in farming villages. The great energy percolating up from the commoners, particularly from the merchant class, could not be contained. A shower of government edicts intended to restrict consumption among farmers and merchants did not prevent ordinary people from striving to live better. In the countryside sharecroppers' lives were a struggle, but farmers who worked their own land could afford to buy more material goods. People traveled far and news of the nation spread quickly. The seeds of a new age, planted in the late Edo period, took hold and flowered in the Meiji Restoration that followed. In the latter decades of the nineteenth century and the first decades of the twentieth, the whole nation was engulfed in a wave of political, social, and economic transformation. The feudal social system was abolished. Strict social taboos that had been enforced by the shogunate were lifted. Commoners' ceremonies and festivals became more elaborate and more formal both in cities and the countryside, in many cases copying customs of the samurai class that had previously been forbidden to them. For instance, in feudal times a bridal procession was the sole prerogative of the daughter of a samurai; now substantial families who had been of commoner status staged elaborate bridal processions in their villages. During this period great numbers of wedding and other ceremonial tsutsugaki textiles were produced in the countryside.

During the Meiji period, the introduction of industrial manufacturing totally changed the conditions of Japanese textile culture. As early as the final year of the Edo period (1867), Shimazu Nariakira, lord of Satsuma, had already installed Japan's first automated Jacquard loom in his domain in southern Kyushu. (It is said he wanted it to weave sails for his ships.) Water-powered spinning and weaving factories were established in the Satsuma capital city, Kagoshima, during the first years of the Meiji period.[3] Local cotton cultivation was dealt a death blow when it was discovered that the short-fiber Japanese cotton was not suitable for machine spinning and weaving. Long staple raw cotton and cotton thread were soon imported in large quantities from China, India, and the United States. By the early years of the twentieth century, local cotton cultivation, hand spinning, and hand weaving had all drastically declined in the face of a rising tide of inexpensive machine-made cotton cloth. In village after village the once pervasive thumping sound of home looms disappeared. Bright colors of chemical dyes replaced the subtle shades of natural dyes. Indigo dyers closed their shops and were forced to find new jobs. People did not want old-fashioned textiles. Bright-colored, machine-printed floral patterns were up-to-date and cranes, tortoises, and the phoenix were forgotten. People stopped ordering hand-crafted celebratory tsutsugaki textiles. By the end of the Taisho period (1912–26), in the mid-1920s, few craftsmen remained who practiced the traditional cotton tsutsugaki craft. The entire tradition was nearing extinction when the first studies of Japanese folk crafts were begun by Yanagi and other urban scholars. Today, a number of urban artist-craftsmen employ tsutsugaki techniques in their individual works of textile art. These are deliberate, personal artistic expressions and not products of the anonymous, collective country textile tradition within which the old cotton tsutsugaki were made. A handful of artisan-dyers follow traditional tsutsugaki techniques of production, but only one family in Izumo, Shimane Prefecture, continues to make traditional tsutsugaki textiles for ceremonial use (and these are limited to wedding furoshiki). The country tradition of cotton tsutsugaki cannot be revived, for it expressed a society, a place, and a time, all of which are lost irrevocably.

Function

In agricultural Japan, elaborate ceremonies marked new stages in human life and the change of seasons. The crisis events of marriage, birth, and death indicated significant alterations in people's lives and were a cause for apprehension about the future, even when they were mixed with joy. Lengthy and elaborate festivities occupied the "liminal," or border, time between old and new social conditions. The festivities focused attention on the change that was occurring and they prepared people in the community to accept it. Ceremonial gifts of cotton tsutsugaki textiles played an important role in these events. Their bold designs, created for the families involved, were deliberately conspicuous. By calling attention to themselves, the textiles were confirmation that the ceremonial event was significant and unusual. Small or inconspicuous gifts would have been ineffectual.

The group of country tsutsugaki textiles that has best survived from the late Edo and Meiji periods relates to weddings. Within this group, futonji and yogi stand out in number and quality, a fact that is reflected in the choice of textiles that are brought together here. Two other outstanding textile bridal gifts were furoshiki, and yutan, covers for bureaus and chests.

In nineteenth-century rural Japan the giving of ceremonial tsutsugaki wedding gifts was an established way of demonstrating family status. During the elaborate marriage ceremonies, gifts were especially evident in the highly public bridal procession, one aspect of conspicuous display borrowed from samurai marriage ceremonies. In earlier times a young man invariably married a young woman from his own village, someone he knew and had probably chosen himself. Normally the choice of a bride had to be approved by the powerful "young man's group" (*waka-monogumi*) of the groom's village. All men from around the ages of fifteen to thirty belonged, and one of its major functions was to arrange marriages for its members. One reason that the custom of holding elaborate wedding ceremonies arose in the countryside during the Edo period was that parents felt they had to please the waka-monogumi and assure its approval of the marriage.[1] Out-marrying was rare and usually discouraged. However, by the nineteenth century marriages arranged by a go-between and linking families who might live in different villages largely replaced the old traditional love match. In the typical arranged marriage bride and groom had not met before the wedding or were only slightly acquainted. It was truly a precarious undertaking for the inexperienced bride to move into the home of her unknown husband's family. It was important to her acceptance, and to the pride of her family, that she be accompanied by a trousseau of valuable and impressive wedding gifts. Parents provided a daughter with as many gifts as they could afford: chests and bureaus, kimono and sash, bedding, and textiles of various kinds, many of which were tsutsugaki textiles. The textiles were decorated with auspicious symbols of happiness and long life and with the family's identifying crest.

In Izumo, where a great many wedding tsutsugaki momen were produced, an average farm girl and the female members of her family spun the cotton and wove the cloth out of which the tsutsugaki textiles in her trousseau were made. The women took the cloth pieces to the local dye shop where artisans drew and dyed the auspicious motifs that would decorate them. The final sewing was also done by the bride, her mother, and other women in the family. The work took six months to a year. On the wedding day, the bride and a train of helpers carrying her trousseau of gifts moved in a grand procession to the place of her husband's home. Tsutsugaki covering cloths of deep indigo blue were carefully draped over new paulownia wood chests and bureaus. Clothes and household objects were wrapped in tsutsugaki furoshiki and carried on a palanquin covered by another cloth that boasted large crests of the bride's family. The young men who carried the gifts were clad in specially made tsutsugaki jackets of indigo-dyed cotton provided by the bride's family. The procession might pass between rice fields along grass-grown dikes or cross hills with the bride riding high on a horse whose back was covered with a tsutsugaki cloth marked with crests. Or the bridal party might float by boat downriver to her new home, the boatman wearing for the occasion a tsutsugaki jacket displaying the bride's crest. The bridal procession meant more than simply traveling to one's destination; it was an occasion to publicly display through conspicuous trappings of ceremonial tsutsugaki momen textiles the pride, status, love, and support of the bride's family in her new life undertaking.

On the bridal nights bride and groom slept under beautifully decorated *futon* (bed cover; also refers to matching sleeping pallet—both stuffed with raw cotton) or covered themselves with yogi bearing auspicious longevity motifs. Afterward, this bedding was treated with special care, normally stored and only brought out for the use of important guests. It is not hard to imagine that the brilliant images of cheerful plums, peonies, and auspicious tortoises and cranes on the bedding provided comfort and encouragement to the young bride. When futon came into general use, probably in the seventeenth century, they brought undreamed of comfort to villagers who normally slept on straw spread on bare earth, covered only by the clothes they wore during the day.[2] Normally only the top futon was made with a cover of tsutsugaki material, but occasionally the bottom futon was covered as well. Futon were made in varying widths, counted by the number of panels or strips of cloth of which they

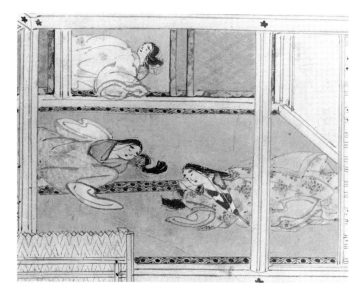

1. Court ladies sleeping under kimono; Kamakura period. From Events in the Life of Kōbō Daishi (Kōbō daishi gyōjō emaki), *scroll, late 13th to early 14th century. (Collection of Honolulu Academy of Arts.)*

2. A tsutsugaki fitted chest cover decorated with a Zingiber (myōga) crest. Possibly from Izumo. (Yuasa Hachirō Memorial Museum, Mitaka.)

were made. A panel was traditionally twelve to thirteen inches wide. Sleeping pallets were usually three panels wide (about 36″ × 60″). *Yono* (four-panel) bed covers (about 65″ × 70″) were covered by a four-panel tsutsugaki cloth surrounded by a six to eight inch border of indigo-blue lining material. *Itsununo* (five-width) bed covers (about 60″ × 70″) were covered by a five-panel piece of tsutsugaki material and were unbordered.[3]

The yogi is a stuffed bed cover made in the shape of a kimono. The use of yogi began in the early years of the Edo period, a reminder of the simple old custom of using a kimono as a night cover.[4] Although a yogi looks like a kimono, it is quite a bit larger, usually about seventy inches long and from sleeve to sleeve sixty-three inches wide. Often the extra width is obtained by inserting an additional center panel, about six inches wide, into the back of the yogi. A triangular gusset at the bottom of the sleeve, seldom found in a standard kimono, gives extra space for arm move-

3. A cotton tsutsugaki wrapping cloth tied at two ends, showing crane crest under knot. From Izumo: Meiji period.

4. A tsutsugaki cloth tied at four ends. From northern Japan; Meiji period. (This and preceding piece from a private collection, Honolulu.)

ment. In the winter time a yogi provides excellent protection against the cold; because of its shape it fits tightly around the shoulders and neck. To offer an elderly guest a yogi was a mark of respect.

A ceremonial yutan was intended to cover, protect, and beautify an important gift. Therefore it was usually made with the size and shape of the gift in mind. Yutan were made to snugly fit and cover the top and four sides of bureaus and chests used to hold clothing. In the case of a bureau, the front panel of the cover hung free so it could be lifted to open the drawers. A yutan made to drape over the ridge pole of a palanquin on which gifts were carried, was a large square of cloth, uncut and unfitted. Yutan were usually decorated with family crests and sometimes with pictorial designs.

A furoshiki is a wrapping and carrying cloth that may be of almost any size— from a foot to as much as five feet on a side. It is a simple, square piece of cloth that can have a thousand uses. In premodern Japan, more than boxes or bags or other containers, an object was wrapped in a furoshiki to protect it, especially when it was being carried from place to place. A furoshiki was lightweight, soft, reusable, folded into a small space when not used, and the tied ends made a good handle for carrying. The Japanese custom of wrapping things in a square of cloth seems to go back as early as the Heian period (794–1185), but the word furoshiki is said to derive from a special bathing custom attributed to the reign of the third Ashikaga shogun, Yoshimitsu (1358–1408). Yoshimitsu invited his lords to bathe together at his residence in Kyoto. Each brought a square of cloth marked with his family crest to spread on the floor while changing clothes and to wrap his clothes while bathing.[5] From this came the name furoshiki, "bath spread." Commoners in the Edo period took up the custom of carrying their bathing clothes to and from the public bath wrapped in a square cloth thus popularizing furoshiki as an item of daily use.[6] Merchants and peddlers found furoshiki to be extremely useful in business. Merchandise was wrapped in large, strong cotton furoshiki tied at the ends and hoisted on the back for carrying. These furoshiki were commonly dyed in tsutsugaki or katazome technique and displayed a large crest of the store or firm. Eventually furoshiki were used by people of all social classes and today furoshiki still remain virtually indispensable in Japanese daily life.

Ceremonial tsutsugaki furoshiki played a particularly important role in rural marriage celebrations. The tsutsugaki furoshiki made in Izumo are well known for their excellent designs and workmanship. A bridal set consisted of three rectangular furoshiki (not square in this case) of graduated size—four, three, and two kimono widths, respectively. The largest was about fifty-two by fifty-six inches and the smallest twenty-six by twenty-eight inches. They were dyed in natural brown, yellow, or, most often, indigo blue. Yellow in Izumo was often the bride's color and brown or blue the groom's. A centered family crest surrounded by large auspicious motifs was a common design. Other furoshiki were divided in half diagonally and each half dyed a different color, with auspicious motifs on each. Often the groom's family ordered large numbers of small indigo-dyed furoshiki marked with the family crest. Each guest was presented with small gifts, including foods considered felicitous for the occasion, wrapped in one of these furoshiki. The furoshiki protected the gifts and made a neat bundle for easy carrying. Even today it remains customary to wrap an important gift in a furoshiki, though the cloth may be machine-woven silk or nylon. A common sight in modern Japan is a group of men and women returning from a wedding ceremony, each carrying an identical furoshiki, usually deep purple and printed with auspicious characters and a family crest, containing the gifts of food and mementos received from the host family.

Other types of cotton tsutsugaki were given as gifts celebrating childbirth and festive events in a child's life. As with bridal tsutsugaki gifts they were made or purchased by the parents of the child's mother. This old and interesting custom probably began with the love marriages of earlier times when a bride lived in her parents' home and gave birth to her first child there. The husband visited but did not live with his bride. Though married, she continued to provide her parents with valuable labor. Thus, for both practical and emotional reasons, it was natural for the mother's parents to feel responsible for providing the many things needed for the baby's birth and early care. In later times a bride who lived in her husband's home customarily returned home in the last month of pregnancy so she could deliver her child in the warmth of her own family. There are good reasons, then, why the custom of maternal grandparents providing birth gifts remained strong in rural Japan into the modern era. If a family was prominent many gifts of high quality would be provided as a matter of pride and to demonstrate family status.

Birth-related tsutsugaki textiles from the Izumo area are especially splendid and in some ways unique. Many baby towels, baby-carrying sashes, diapers, and foot towels (*ashifuki*), all practical gifts, have survived. Among these the baby towels are most interesting. Typically they are rectangular in shape, sewn of two or three panels of traditional kimono material, dyed in indigo blue, and decorated with colorful auspicious motifs. One of the special characteristics of baby towels from Izumo is a bright red patch of color—traditionally dyed with madder (*akane*) or safflower (*benibana*)

5. A tsutsugaki baby diaper made of two layers of cloth reinforced with sashiko stitches. From Izumo; Meiji period. (Collection of Yuasa Hachirō Memorial Museum, Mitaka.)

in a triangular shape—that appears in the upper part of the design and most often in the right top corner. The color red was believed to expel evil and prevent smallpox, a devastating childhood disease for which no cure was known in Edo times. There is basis for this belief. The fact is most natural dyes used in the countryside came from plants that were known to have medicinal properties. In the pharmacopeia of Chinese medicine which was practiced in Japan, madder was prescribed for bleeding, jaundice, or rheumatism and safflower for fever, high blood pressure, and irregular menses. Red was also very special because it was one of the colors prohibited to commoners during the Edo period.[7] Red was therefore considered a precious color, allied with power and status. The towel's red area was only used to wipe the baby's face, while other parts of the towel were used to wipe the baby's body.

Delightful ceremonial tsutsugaki baby-carrying sashes, diapers, and foot towels also come from Izumo. The carrying sash is a long narrow strip of cloth made from a single width of kimono material. It is traditional for a mother to carry her baby on her back, held firmly but gently against her body in a sling. The sling's middle section, which supports the baby, has a family crest and the two ends have auspicious motifs that appear on the bow that is tied in front. This simple sash freed a mother's hands so she could keep her baby next to her while working in the fields or doing domestic chores. Traditional tsutsugaki baby diapers, often decorated with anchor or shrimp designs, came in a set of seven rectangular pieces: one large diaper (ca. 23″ × 35″) and six small ones (ca. 12″ × 22″). Usually two layers of cloth were stitched together for strength. Each side might have different design motifs. Finally, small-sized towels were made especially to wipe a baby's feet. The Izumo foot towels are known for their puckish design of two white baby footprints on a dark indigo background. In addition to being practical, tsutsugaki baby towels, sashes, and diapers served as auspicious tokens welcoming and celebrating a new life. They became customary gifts from the bride's family to the groom's family.

Tall, vertical banners are another striking manifestation of ceremonial tsutsugaki. In medieval Japan towering banners, often emblazoned with large family crests, identified samurai clans during battle and marked the war camps of their generals. During three centuries of peace in the Edo period, banners became heraldic devices for proud samurai families. The custom of flying tall tsutsugaki banners decorated with family crests on Boy's Day (the fifth day of the fifth lunar month) probably began among samurai.[8] Originally in the countryside the May festival celebrated the first rice planting of the year and young girls who were to set out the rice shoots gathered together in one house, the roof of which was covered with *shōbu* (a type of iris) intended to drive away evil. The word shōbu also means to foster martial arts and on this day boys engaged in war games and contests, symbolizing competition in rice growing. In time the fifth of May became a festival for boys. The sight of a waving banner, rising fifteen to twenty feet into the air above a village house, was an unequivocal announcement of a boy child in the family and the wish that the child would grow up to be a strong, healthy man. Once again the ceremonial tsutsugaki banner was likely to be supplied by a boy's maternal grandparents or it might be the gift of another relative.

Long tsutsugaki banners were seamed together of two widths of kimono material, short banners of a single width. The cloth was hung vertically from the arm of a bamboo pole; a series of cloth loops running down the length of the pole held the banner in place when the wind blew strong. Figures of warriors made up the main motif and often a large family crest was placed proudly above this design. The patterns were outlined with paste resist in tsutsugaki technique and the colors filled in by painting with pigments. Very rarely was a banner dip-dyed in indigo; the background was usually white. The tradition of making and flying banners on Boy's Day to celebrate a boy child's future manhood remains strong today. Another kind of tsutsugaki pennant, smaller and brightly colored but also called nobori, has traditionally been made for fishing vessels. Even

6. *Boy's Day banner; Meiji period (see Plate 43 for detail). (Collection of Honolulu Academy of Arts.)*

7. *Women hiding their faces in public in kazuki. From* Scenes Inside and Outside of Kyoto (Rakuchū rakugaizu), *screen, early 17th century. (Collection of Honolulu Academy of Arts; gift of Mrs. Charles M. Cooke, Sr.)*

now, a ship heading back to port with lines of bright pennants snapping in the wind from its rigging signals the news of a good catch to families waiting on shore.

The maiwai is a unique ceremonial tsutsugaki jacket that used to be worn by fishermen along the coast of the Boso Peninsula near Tokyo. Maiwai means "a million congratulations" (or with a different ideograph "dance of congratulation"). Originally made of hand-spun, indigo-dyed cotton material decorated with colorful ocean scenes and auspicious motifs, maiwai were at first the identifying garb of a ship owner or captain of a fishing crew. The jacket was a symbol of status, worn only on New Year's Day and other occasions of a ceremonial nature. In the course of time, however, ship owners began to give maiwai to their crews as a special bonus when they surpassed the expected year's fishing catch. Maiwai were made in increasingly large numbers during the early part of this century. In order to replicate the same pattern in large quantities on jackets, freehand tsutsugaki drawing had to be abandoned as too labor intensive. The faster process of stencil dyeing, which is more appropriate to mass production, gradually replaced tsutsugaki technique. Almost all maiwai produced in the late Meiji and Taisho periods (ca. 1900–1925) were made by stencil dyeing.[9]

Large tsutsugaki patterns also decorated a garment which had the unique function of concealing the head. The custom of using a special kimono, called *kazuki* or *katsugi*, as a head covering has survived down to the present day. Since Heian times Japanese women have worn head coverings to conceal their faces when going out of doors. Early practice—simply lifting a standard garment over the head—is illustrated in the *Fan-Shaped Book of the Lotus Sutra (Senmen hokekyō sasshi)*, of the Heian period,[10] and in the thirteenth-century scroll, *Pictorial Life of Saint Ippen (Ippen shōnin eden)*, for example.[11] The modest gesture of Heian nobility was probably adopted by commoners during the Kamakura period (1185–1392). During the early Edo period a specially cut kimono was invented to hide the head. The collar was

8. *Hemp tsutsugaki curtain; probably Meiji period, with plum crest and sailboats. (Collection of Serizawa Keisuke Art Museum, Shizuoka. Photo: Barbara Stephan)*

lowered so that a pocket of material was created above the collar in which the head could be concealed. This type of kazuki used by commoners was usually of hemp, as illustrated by the example from northern Japan (Plate 45), and less often of silk. A government order prohibited wearing kazuki within the city of Edo (ca. 1658–1661). Apparently an assassin who tried to kill Izunokami Matsudaira, a member of the shogun's council of elders, disguised himself under a kazuki.[12] But elsewhere in the country women continued to wear kazuki especially for such formal occasions as weddings and funerals. In northern Japan kazuki were still made and occasionally worn until recent times. As late as 1943, the case of a bride entering the home of her new parents-in-law with her face respectfully hidden in a kazuki is reported. When the garment is removed the bride makes a sudden, theatrical appearance. The same kazuki would be worn during a funeral, the left sleeve of the kimono covering the head and the hanging right sleeve tucked into the sash.[13]

Throughout the Edo period other types of tsutsugaki textiles were created in large quantities that had special, but prosaic, functions. Every commercial establishment was clearly identified by a boldly designed curtain that hung from the front eave of its shop or store. Sometimes it was broad enough to cover the entire building front; usually it concealed only the entrance. Its hanging length was one to five or more feet. Traditional stores today still hang conspicuous tsutsugaki curtains, in part to indicate their continuity with the past. The typical noren is visually striking. Dyed a solid dark color, the business's logo or crest or name stands out sharply in white. The design must be arresting, for it advertises the store. It is the establishment's trademark and is passed from generation to generation. The mundane purpose of a noren is to keep dust and rain from entering and to provide shade in the heat of summer. Hanging at eye level it keeps the gawker from peering inside at will, yet can be brushed aside by the entering customer. A noren is made of separate hanging strips sewed together at the top, inviting a person to enter between them. Symbolically a noren identifies an entrance and welcomes a visitor to enter; at the same time it indicates a boundary that must be deliberately passed. The ambivalent nature of the noren seems especially Japanese if compared to the absolute closure and solid barrier that is represented by a Western door.

Noren of various sizes were also hung inside homes between rooms or in entryways (*zashiki noren*, room curtain). In the Kaga area of Ishikawa Prefecture, a long cotton tsutsugaki room curtain, called *soto noren* (outside noren), was customarily hung between the "outer" front guest room and the family rooms at the back of, that is, inside, the house. It elegantly concealed the family's mundane activities from a guest's sight but did not interfere with air circulation. And the large white crest on its center panel conspicuously announced to any visitor the family's status.

Although tsutsugaki textiles were widely used in rural Japan during the Edo period, their special power and their original importance derive from carefully delimited functions. These are functions related to auspicious occasions for which the bold motifs and strong dyed colors of tsutsugaki are considered highly appropriate. The dynamic pictorial images of tsutsugaki momen call welcome attention to these crucial events in rural life.

Motifs

Most of the tsutsugaki textiles displayed here were made for celebrations and their motifs are generally of an auspicious nature. One of the most common tsutsugaki motifs is the combination of pine, bamboo, and plum, known as *shōchikubai*. The three trees are ancient symbols of longevity, fidelity, and integrity. The pine is ever green, lives to be a thousand years old, and is the dwelling place of gods. The bamboo bends under heavy snow yet never breaks. It is the symbol of endurance and resilience, a place where a god descends to earth, and a participant in religious ceremonies. Each New Year Japanese still decorate the gate or front entrance of their home with *kadomatsu* (gate pine), an auspicious decoration of pine and bamboo through which the god of the new year may descend to bestow his blessing on the household. The plum, courageously blooming in February's cold before any other flower, symbolizes bravery. It is associated with wisdom, for it is said that the plum blooms when human knowledge is advanced. In the Confucian classics the three trees are cited as models of the virtues that a man should follow when faced with the adversities of life. They are commonly known in Japan as "the three friends of the cold season" (*saikan no san'yū*).[1] We might also call them "the three friends of less fortunate times." When, in the Edo period, tsutsugaki textiles were important gifts at weddings, the thoughts of longevity, perseverance, and fidelity associated with shōchikubai made it an exceptionally popular, and appropriate, design.

Two animals familiar in Japanese decorative arts, crane and tortoise (*tsuru kame*), frequently appear together in tsutsugaki textiles. The crane is known in Japan as a symbol of beauty. The stark contrast of black and white on its body, the bright red spot on its head, the delicacy of its form, and its elegant posture exemplify the Japanese taste for simplicity and serenity. In Japan the crane has qualities of spirituality, courtesy, and punctiliousness. The crane occasionally appears as a heroine in folk stories where, disguised, she serves as a beautiful, obedient, and hard-working wife to a mortal man. The popular expression "one cry of a crane" (*tsuru no hitokoe*)

*9. Pine, bamboo, plum motif
(detail of Plate 1).*

*10. Crane motif (detail of Plate 25) and tortoise
motif (detail of Plate 17, right tortoise).*

means the final voice of authority, because the crane's cry is so majestic and powerful. The crane was portrayed in early Japanese art flying with a pine sprig in its beak (decorative objects stored in the Shōsōin Treasure House, Nara, depict its Persian prototype—birds carrying jewelry, flowers, and branches in their beaks).[2] By Heian times the crane was associated in art with longevity because of the belief that it lived a thousand years. The crane was a symbol of good fortune and it was natural that crane designs would become important in the tsutsugaki repertory of motifs.

The tortoise is a constant companion of the crane in story and in art. According to Chinese legend the tortoise is associated with north, is one of the four sacred animals (together with the dragon, kirin, and phoenix), is a symbol of stability and good fortune, and lives for ten thousand years.[3] In ancient China it was widely believed that a tortoise supports the heavens. It was the carrier of precious things and a messenger of good omen, particularly the words of gods. The earliest tortoise design on a Japanese textile is preserved on the famous seventh-century fabric known as the Heavenly Embroidery (*Tenjukoku shūchō*), made to honor the life of the imperial prince, Shōtoku (d. 622). Originally the piece contained one hundred tortoises, each a messenger bearing on its shell part of a commemorative tribute.[4] Studying the cracks that appear in a heated tortoise shell was a method of divination practiced in China since ancient times. Perhaps in part because of their connotation of magical knowledge of the future, geometric tortoise-shell patterns have been widely popular in Japanese art. On tsutsugaki textiles the tortoise design called *minogame* (caped tortoise) is especially common. The design shows a type of tortoise that carried

11. Phoenix motif (detail of Plate 4).

exceptionally good fortune, with long "tails" trailing behind in the water which represented seaweed attached to the shell.

In Chinese legend all these felicitous trees and animals are associated with Mount Hōrai, a paradise of everlasting life. Here the crane lives; pine, bamboo, and plum flourish; and a tortoise supports the mountain, and the world, on its back. The Hōrai motif is seen in Japanese art of the Heian period. A beautiful example is a lacquer box for a priest's robe, now in the Tokyo National Museum, that shows a rugged mountain standing on the back of a tortoise that floats in the midst of the ocean. Cranes fly across the sky carrying pine branches in their bills. During the Kamakura period the Chinese mountain disappears from the design and bamboo joins growing Japanese pine trees. In the Muromachi period (1392–1568) plum trees begin to appear as part of the motif, and the typical Japanese image of Mount Hōrai is established, the three auspicious trees and two animals together.[5] Mount Hōrai motifs were extremely popular during the Edo period as symbols of good fortune and long life. Some of the most sophisticated and colorful tsutsugaki wedding textiles contain integrated Mount Hōrai designs: crane and tortoise motifs together with the three friends of winter—pine, bamboo, and plum.

Another combined motif commonly found on auspicious tsutsugaki textiles is paulownia-and-phoenix (*kiri hōō*). The paulownia (*kiri*) probably came to Japan from China. In early summer large bell-shaped flowers of a pale lavender hue spread a sweet fragrance in the air around the trees. Paulownia grows rapidly and it was once the custom to plant a paulownia when a girl was born so its wood could be used to make her wedding bureau. The light, strong wood is prized for making musical instruments, *koto* and *biwa*, as well as utilitarian objects such as clogs and boxes. The paulownia leaf was reserved as the crest of the emperor until the four-teenth century, when it was awarded to certain military conquerors as a special privilege. In the first such case Emperor Godaigo granted the crest to the Ashikaga

12. Chinese lion motif (detail of Plate 9).

shogun Takauji (1305–58). Two centuries later Toyotomi Hideyoshi (1536–98), self-made peasant-warrior ruler, received from the imperial court the right to use the paulownia leaf in his family crest.[6] The popularity of paulownia-leaf motifs spread to all classes during the Edo period. The phoenix (*hōō*) and the paulownia tree are intimately associated in Chinese legend—the phoenix will only alight on the branches of this tree. The mythical phoenix lives solely on holy sweet water and the seeds of bamboo; it flies with the clouds, and it is seen only at the time of a great event such as the appearance of a truly virtuous ruler. It is a composite of many animals, a symbol of peace and the rising sun, a bird whose song is particularly musical and auspicious. Because the phoenix is the female counterpart of the male dragon and its varied colored feathers represent the traditional virtues—truthfulness, propriety, righteousness, benevolence, and sincerity—it is an auspicious bridal motif, hence popular in tsutsugaki textiles.[7]

The triply auspicious combined motif of paulownia, phoenix, and bamboo, a significant woven textile design in ancient times, was reserved for decorating the garments of Japanese emperors. Phoenix forms woven into emperors' robes of the Edo period are rigid, formalized patterns, but the dyed phoenix motifs that were so popular in tsutsugaki textiles of the same period show huge, stately birds sporting beautiful feathers that spread outward like colorful ribbons. On tsutsugaki bridal bed covers and sleeping kimono the phoenix most often appears together with paulownia leaves, flowers, and bamboo.

Chinese lion and peonies (*karajishi botan*) form another traditional combination motif that decorates wedding tsutsugaki bed covers. As its name suggests, China is the direct source of these decorative figures, although the lion motif probably ultimately derives from Persian art forms.[8] Peonies were used as medicine and were the symbol of wealth and prosperity in China. In Japan, lion and peonies have been associated with Buddhism since early times. They were popular motifs among the

Heian nobility and in the Kamakura period warrior armor was decorated with them. Colorful peonies suited the taste of newly risen warrior-rulers Oda Nobunaga (1534–82) and Toyotomi Hideyoshi. During the brilliant Momoyama period (1568–1603) that encompasses their reigns, large peony designs were prominent in architectural reliefs and were incorporated in wall and screen paintings. Lion and peony motifs found in tsutsugaki textiles seem to be closely related to the Noh drama *Stone Bridge* (*Shakkyō*), one of a small number of celebratory plays in the dramatic repertory. The play dramatizes the legend of Jakushō, a Japanese monk who is stopped before a stone bridge while visiting Mount Seiryō in China. He is told the land beyond is ruled by Monju (Mañjuśrī), the bodisattva of wisdom who sits at the left hand of Buddha and rides a lion. A lion appears and dances energetically among peony blossoms to celebrate longevity and a felicitous life.[9] This motif of a lion dancing amidst peony flowers is often brocaded in Noh costumes used for this play. The woven lions, although elegant, remain purely decorative designs. The lions drawn by country tsutsugaki dyers, on the other hand, wonderfully capture the vigorous movement of the stage lion dancing. The lions are amazingly alert and animated. Placed in diagonal positions, some tsutsugaki lions appear to be caught in a moment of flying or an extended leap. The face, innocent or fierce, is full of expression. Following yin and yang cosmology, a lion is the masculine manifestation of energy while peonies are the feminine manifestation of beauty and sexuality. The lion-peony motif is therefore especially appropriate for the sacred occasion on which a man and a woman join together to begin a new life. (The charming butterflies that tease and lure the lion in Noh and Kabuki performances of *Stone Bridge* do not appear in tsutsugaki designs.)

The repertory of tsutsugaki motifs is large. Artisans in the countryside who made tsutsugaki momen for local use were not restricted by protocol or rigid customs of an elite. Nor were they obligated, as urban artists often were, to follow current artistic fads. Using pictorial images familiar to rural people, country tsutsugaki artisans delighted in working out interesting and varied designs. Against a typical deep blue background flowers bloom, arabesques swirl, sparrows fly, loving Mandarin ducks float on a stream, and carp swim under a splashing waterfall. Ordinary images carry hidden significance: a ship anchor holds a bride secure in her new life; the bent tails of shrimp recall the bent backs of those fortunate to live into old age; designs of dried abalone represent auspicious offerings. Objects of daily living—tea-ceremony utensils, kitchen tools, and vegetables—appear on tsutsugaki textiles in the most spontaneous manner. Nor is mischievous humor absent. Fecundity is humorously suggested by a long forked radish.[10] The innocent, childlike face of the Zen patriarch Daruma peeks from a scroll design.

A notable feature of cotton tsutsugaki design is the dramatic use of family crests. Crests, like so many aspects of Japanese culture, can be traced back to Chinese examples, in this case emblems of authority. The *Later Chronicles of Japan* (*Shoku nihongi*), a court history, records how, in 701, banners of the Japanese Emperor Mommu were decorated with sun, moon, dragon, peacock, tortoise, tiger, and crow, all Chinese imperial symbols. During the Heian period emblems came to identify each important court family, the specific crest chosen to express the aesthetic taste of a

13. Above left: *carp motif on tsutsugaki bed cover. (Collection of Araki Kazuo, Kagawa Prefecture.)*

14. Above: *shrimp motif with orange flower* (tachibana) *and pine on tsutsugaki bureau cover. (Collection of Nippon Mingeikan.)*

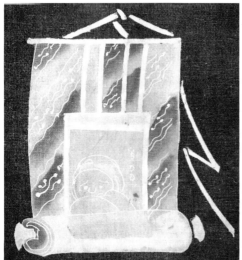

15. *Daruma on vertical scroll painting (detail of Plate 19. Photo: Arnold Sprague).*

family. Many of these were no longer Chinese derived. It is said that traffic jams on the streets of the Heian capital led lords to emblazon ox carts with the family crest as a means of locating them in the crush of hundreds of similar vehicles.[11] Samurai families in Japan's age of high feudalism (14th–16th centuries) ostentatiously displayed family crests as a mark of, usually new-found, status and power. In battle, a warrior boasted to the enemy of his lineage or name by emblazoning banner, armor, helmet, trappings, and equipment with his personal crest. The propensity of samurai to display the family crest on clothing, flags, boxes, utensils, buildings—almost any usable surface—became even more pronounced during the three peaceful centuries of the Edo period. Unable to prove their worth in battle, families used the crest as a statement of status within samurai society. Many new designs were created and by the

16. *Cotton tsutsugaki bridal lantern cover from Izumo with double falcon crest*
(takanoha). *17. Cotton tsutsugaki bridal umbrella cover from Izumo with*
Zingiber crest. (Both collection of Yuasa Hachirō Memorial Museum, Mitaka.)

mid-seventeenth century the design of samurai family crests was officially cod-
ified.

During the Edo period commoners, willy-nilly, took up family crests (pattern
books of more than 3,000 crests were published). Kabuki actors and famous courtesans invented and popularized scores of arresting family crests in the seventeenth
and eighteenth centuries. Rich city merchants displayed family crests on their products, their clothes, and on the curtains hung before their shops as a form of advertising. Merchants dressed their employees in jackets with a large crest of the firm
prominently dyed on the back. Crest fever eventually reached the countryside. A
prominent farmer could wear a black kimono decorated with five family crests on
formal occasions, just as his city relatives could. The original function of the crest—
to distinguish one family from another—still operated in the countryside but on a
casual basis: a crest might be chosen because the design was attractive, or it was
borrowed from another family, or a new one was created to suit individual tastes.
Groups unrelated by blood also began to use crests to identify their members (in
one case, everyone in the village took the same crest).[12] In those rural communities
where family ties were strong, displaying the family crest on festive occasions was a
significant means of affirming blood kinship and loyalty to the family line.

Crests on ceremonial tsutsugaki textiles reflect this tradition. As if to emphasize a
family's importance, tsutsugaki crests are usually of very large size. Crests eighteen
inches in diameter are not uncommon and some are even larger. They appear in
various positions—the center, top, and corners of a piece. Such extremely large crests
may appear on tsutsugaki textiles alone but more commonly they are combined
with pictorial designs. The crest will often be the focus of the entire textile design,
even when the overall design is of some complexity. Although it may seem that
crests are being treated purely as a part of a decorative pattern by tsutsugaki artisans
and dyers, on the finest ceremonial tsutsugaki textiles that were made in nineteenth-

century rural Japan, the crest was also a statement of family solidarity, proclaimed in public on ceremonial occasions. On bridal bed coverings, on ceremonial furoshiki, on Boy's Day banners, the prominent display of a family crest of paulownia leaf, or melon, or wisteria, or crane, or crossed feathers, was an important affirmation of the continuity of a family through the generations, of its honor and its pride.

Tsutsugaki Technique

In a narrow sense, the word tsutsugaki means the process of applying a paste-resist pattern to cloth prior to dyeing. The "writing" instrument for applying the paste and the technique of application are unique. Thick rice paste is held in a cone-shaped tube fashioned of handmade Japanese paper which has been strengthened by the application of persimmon juice. The tube is eight to ten inches long. A brass tip or nib (bamboo in the past) controls the flow of paste from the narrow opening when the tube is gently squeezed. The bold patterns and broad lines typical of tsutsugaki textiles are produced by tsutsu fitted with tips that have large openings (flat or round). To make fine lines or delineate details, a tsutsu with a small tip is used. In common usage the term tsutsugaki also generally refers to the major process of making the textile—drawing the rice-paste pattern and dip-dyeing—and to the finished textiles as well.

Tsutsugaki is one of the later types of resist dyeing developed by Japanese artisans. As early as the Nara period (710–94), dye patterns were being produced on fabrics by three different resist processes. Prior to dyeing, cloth was clamped between wooden blocks on which patterns had been carved (kyōkechi), wax patterns were drawn on cloth (rōkechi), or cloth was tightly bound, stitched, or folded to prevent dye from reaching selected areas (kōkechi). Examples of resist-dyed textiles of these three types, attributed to the Nara period, are preserved at the Shōsōin Treasure House in Nara.[1] The first two methods gradually fell into disuse, perhaps because kyōkechi was a difficult technique and the wax for rōkechi was expensive and had to be imported. The third resist method, kōkechi, has been practiced continuously in Japan for more than a millennium: it is widely known today under the name *shibori*. Shibori is a technically simple process capable of producing designs of spontaneous beauty. After flourishing through the Muromachi and Momoyama periods, shibori technique became increasingly elaborate during the Edo period (often combined with embroidery) in response to demands for ever greater embellishment of kimono design.

18. Well-used cones fitted with brass tips, and separate tips of various shapes and sizes. (Photo: Barbara Stephan)

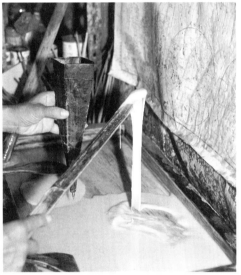

19. Filling a cone with rice paste. (Photo: Barbara Stephan)

20. Drawing a design with rice paste squeezed from a cone. (Photo: Barbara Stephan)

It is not known when rice paste was first used as a resist medium in Japanese textiles. Paste as a resist agent apparently developed in China before it did in Japan. Chinese paste was made of soybean flour, which is not soluble in water.[2] It had to be scraped off with a dull knife and the edges of patterns made with the paste were rough. It is believed that early yūzen textiles were resisted with an insoluble paste (*itchinko*) made of wheat flour, which was a derivative of the Chinese type of paste adopted by Japanese artisans. When paste made of water-soluble rice flour was developed in Japan it had two clear advantages over earlier resist agents: it made a hard edge and it was easily washed away in water after the fabric was dyed. It is also said that rice paste was developed as a substitute for wax, which was difficult to obtain.

Tsutsugaki and katazome (literally pattern dyeing) are the two traditional paste-

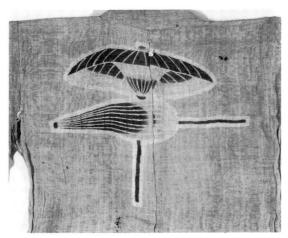

21. Detail of a Noh costume, Muromachi period, showing an umbrella
design, rice-paste-resist dyed. (Collection of Tokyo National Museum.
Photo: Shiono Naoshige, Tokyo National Museum.)

resist processes followed in Japan. Rice-paste resist textiles may have been produced
as early as the Kamakura period, many centuries after the earlier resist methods were
known. For example, the *Mongol Invasions Picture Scroll* (*Mōkoshūrai ekotoba*, ca. 1293)
shows a warrior wearing a formal outer garment (*hitatare*) decorated with a large
family crest. The prominent textile scholar Yamanobe Tomoyuki speculates the
cloth's deep blackish blue color may be the result of dipping in indigo and black dye
(which produced a hue widely popular with samurai, called *kachi* or victory color)
and, since the white of the crest had to be protected from dye penetration in some
fashion, a resist technique with the use of rice paste is possible.[3] The resist method
may have been tsutsugaki, katazome, or some other method.

A surprising number of rice-paste resist textiles from the Muromachi period have
been preserved. A costume of a Noh actor in the collection of the Tokyo National
Museum is dyed with dark blue umbrella motifs on light yellow ground. Scholars
such as Yamanobe, textile authority Kitamura Tetsurō, and Imanaga Seijirō, curator
of decorative arts, Tokyo National Museum, agree the umbrella design was made
by rice-paste resist dyeing, either by freehand tsutsu drawing or by stencil.[4] Kitamura
points to three other garments of the period which appear to have been made by
tsutsugaki technique—a Noh hitatare costume, with flower and *shikishi* (square poem
card) pattern in the collection of Kasuga Shrine, Gifu; a small-sleeved kimono (kosode)[5] with flower and bird pattern, dated 1566, in the Tokyo National Museum;
and a *dōfuku* (man's outer jacket), with snowflake and circle (*yukiwa*) and gingko-leaf
patterns in the collection of the Yoshioka family. In Kitamura's opinion the fine
lines in the kosode and dōfuku patterns are evidence that thin lines of rice paste
(*itomenori*) were hand drawn with a tsutsu.[6] After the application of the paste, pigments were brushed on to create colored areas. Finally, Kamakura Yoshitarō, desig-
nated an Intangible Cultural Asset for textile artistry and known for his scholarship,
describes a tsutsugaki garment he discovered on Amami-Oshima Island, Okinawa

Prefecture. It is documented that the garment was a gift of the Okinawan king in the latter half of the sixteenth century.[7]

Resist dyeing of garments was greatly stimulated during the Edo period by sumptuary edicts that prohibited commoners from wearing luxurious clothing. One of the harshest edicts, in 1683, said that henceforth women could not wear three of the most beautiful and expensive fabrics then being made: *kinsha*, a delicate fabric woven in *sha* (gauze) technique with gold-thread patterns; *nui* embroidery; and *sōkanoko*, a fabric covered with tiny closely spaced circles dyed in shibori technique.[8] Even though this and other edicts were only sporadically enforced, the world of seventeenth century fashion faced the difficult problem of meeting its clients' demands for beautiful garments without obviously flouting the law. Resist-dyed patterns made by tsutsu and stencil provided one answer. Perhaps the greatest advantage of drawing patterns with a tsutsu was that the artisan was free to make whatever design he or she wished. Two particularly important new types of resist-dyed materials and patterns were created by artisans in the early Edo period with the help of tsutsu drawing.

The first new type was a summer kimono of dyed ramie made by a reversal of the usual tsutsugaki process. The entire surface of the kimono was covered on both sides with thick rice paste except for detailed patterns of fine lines that were left untouched. When the cloth was dipped in indigo dye the result was an intricate tracery of thin blue lines on a pure white background. Called chayazome or *chayatsuji*, this striking summer kimono became exceptionally popular among high-ranking samurai women. Making chayazome was demanding, tedious work; if there was the slightest flaw in the paste resist, dye would penetrate onto the white background, ruining the piece. Today this technique is no longer practiced leaving the true process of chayazome and the recipe of the thick paste a mystery. Yūzen, developed by Kyoto artisans, used, in part, tsutsugaki methods. Beautiful, delicately drawn yūzen patterns on silk fabrics were famous through the whole of the Edo period. The term is said to come from the name of a seventeenth-century Kyoto fan painter, Yūzen (or Yūzensai); many familiar yūzen patterns consist of small motifs within framing devices, a pictorial scheme surely derived from fan paintings. In fact, kimono with yūzen characteristics were made before Yūzen's time, but the name is commonly attributed to his influence.[9]

The yūzen process consists of eight steps: 1) mark the patterns in outline with *aobana*, a blue liquid extracted from a plant of the spiderwort family (*tsuyukusa*); 2) using a tsutsu with an extremely narrow tip, cover the lines of the pattern with rice paste; 3) paint the whole cloth with soybean liquid (*gojiru*) (see p. 35); 4) paint the uncovered, inner areas of the design with dyes—or occasionally pigments; 5) cover the painted areas with rice paste; 6) brush on background color; 7) steam the painted fabric to fasten the dye; 8) wash off the paste in water. Yūzen kimono were not dip-dyed and their designs were drawn in meticulous, fine lines—two major differences from cotton tsutsugaki textiles. Because yūzen was a delicate and lengthy process and used silk material, finished kimono were expensive, accessible only to the wealthy and the social elite—samurai, important merchants, and the most successful courtesans and Kabuki actors. Yūzen garments were far beyond the reach of country people.

Durable, practical indigo-dyed cotton clothing and utilitarian textiles became essentials in the lives of people of the countryside during the Edo period. In addition to farm families that did their own dyeing, almost every village had its dye shop (kon'ya or kōya, literally "blue house," indicating indigo) that served local people's needs. Unfortunately, we know little about how the highly artistic freehand tsutsugaki drawing technique entered rural dye culture. Some transmission of yūzen technique to the countryside seems probable and with it the transfer of silk-dyeing methods to cotton (the best fabric allowed rural people by the government). For example, in Kanazawa City in the eighteenth century some indigo-dye shops produced both silk yūzen fabrics (called Kaga yūzen) and dip-dyed cotton tsutsugaki fabrics.[10] But we really don't know whether tsutsugaki drawing developed simultaneously in cities and in the countryside, first in cities, or first in villages. The origins of country tsutsugaki are difficult to detect because the dyers' craft was not an elite activity. Written records about textiles made in villages are few. Craftsmen did not sign their pieces or affix dates (as painters do). The vast majority of textiles that were made no longer exist— a fabric was thrown away when it became worn or old-fashioned. Pieces changed function—a kimono-shaped yogi would be remade into a flat bed cover or a yutan into a curtain, for example—so that the textile we see today may not be in its original form. What is clear is that the craft of making indigo-dyed cotton textiles with tsutsugaki drawing technique was widespread throughout rural Japan by the eighteenth century.

Production of varied styles of ceremonial tsutsugaki momen flourished from late Edo through the Meiji period. Similar textiles were produced in many parts of the country, but some styles tend to be associated with certain areas. It is possible to say, for example, that clear motifs and simple dyeing in one or two shades of indigo were characteristic of tsutsugaki textiles made in Izumo and other parts of western Japan that face the Japan Sea and in Tohoku. Brighter tsutsugaki textiles were popular in far western Japan, especially Kyushu and Shikoku. Some scholars suggest these country tsutsugaki textiles show the influence of colorful Okinawan bingata. (Like yūzen and chayazome, these colorful Okinawan textiles were made for an urban elite.[11]) Brilliant colors were created by brushing pigments (ganryō), usually suspended in a soybean-liquid binder, onto the surface of the fabric in a manner similar to yūzen. A design is outlined in rice paste with a tsutsu and the open design areas are filled in with the desired pigment colors. There is no limit to the number of colors that can be used, although in practice usually five or six is the maximum. Pigments can be painted on selective areas: a single spot of rose color can be painted on a crane's head, for example. After applying the pigments the painted areas are covered with rice paste using a tsutsu and the fabric is then dip-dyed. Banners are colored entirely by painting and are not dip-dyed.

Popular inorganic pigments were mercuric sulfide (shu) for bright reds, iron oxide (bengara) for red-brown, iron hydroxide (ōdo) for dull yellow and ochre, and arsenic trisulfide (kiō or sekiō) for rich yellow. Important organic pigments were juice of the cochineal insect (yōkō) mixed with alum for vivid red-blue, precipitated indigo (aibō) for deep blue, and calligraphy ink—lampblack made of pine soot (sumi).[12] Pigments are opaque and insoluble in water. Because they remain on the fabric surface, they tend to rub off with use. They also stiffen fabric making it generally unsuitable for clothing. Inasmuch as most tsutsugaki textiles were ceremonial, these characteristics of pigments were not a serious handicap.

Tsutsugaki pieces can be identified with regional styles only in a very general way. The personal style of the dyer was probably more important than any regional style. A well-known dyer's works were certain to be used as models and copied by lesser artisans, so that similar works might be produced in distant places in spite of regional traditions. Textiles are light and easily moved, so a tsutsugaki piece found in a certain region of Japan may not have been made there. The custom of giving tsutsugaki textiles as bridal gifts dispersed textiles beyond the areas in which they were made.

The essence of tsutsugaki craft is that each textile is a unique hand-woven, hand-drawn, and hand-dyed creation. When factory technology replaced crafts in this century as the basic mechanism for producing people's clothing and textiles, knowledge of tsutsugaki momen production rapidly disappeared. By the 1920s only a handful of country artisans continued to make ceremonial tsutsugaki momen even on a small scale. Today one family continues to make ceremonial cotton tsutsugaki in traditional style in Izumo City, Shimane Prefecture, a few miles from the coastline of the Japan Sea. In order to illustrate the tsutsugaki process, I will describe how this family carries on its work.[13]

The Nagata family home and working place is an unexceptional wooden building in the center of Izumo City strategically fronting the Takase River, a small stream that provides the water necessary for their tsutsugaki work. When the Nagata dye firm was founded in 1887, Izumo City was famous for tsutsugaki-textile production and the new shop was one of fifty-nine commercial dyeing operations. The number of dye firms fell to twenty-eight in the mid-1920s, eight in the 1930s, and two in 1983. The Nagata firm has survived because all members of the family, now in its fourth generation, are dedicated to their craft. The family head is Nagata Yasushi, grandson of the founder of the firm; he was taught tsutsugaki by his father. The flow of work is under his direction but each member of the family takes part: his wife Reiko, Yukiyoshi his brother, and his son Shigenobu. Their work day begins at 8:30 A.M. and continues until 6 P.M. Although each tsutsugaki-textile family had its own method of dye preparation, rice-paste formula, and dyeing techniques, the Nagata family's work process is as follows.

First, a length of cotton fabric of traditional width (13″) is scoured. This is the task of Reiko, Nagata's wife. She boils the fabric in water to rid the fibers of oil, warp sizing, and natural waxes that would interfere with dye absorption. She rinses the fabric and dries it in the sun. Then Nagata pounds it on a wooden fulling block (*kinuta ban*) with a wooden mallet until it becomes soft and pliable. Second, the fabric is cut and sewn according to the customer's order. This is usually the wife's task as well. Today, most orders are for ceremonial furoshiki and that is what is described here; a cloth square is made by sewing together several widths of fabric. Third, the cloth is stretched tight to provide a smooth surface for the design. Nagata uses two- to three-inch-wide split bamboo stretchers (*shinshi*) that do not bend too easily and these are fastened to opposite corners of the cloth. Fourth, a light outline of the design is drawn on the cloth with pencil or charcoal (*mokutan*). Fifth, the tsutsu is

22. Nagata Yukiyoshi drawing a design with rice
paste and cone; Izumo. (Photo: Senshoku arufā)

prepared for use. Nagata's brother Yukiyoshi usually applies the rice paste. He has
an assortment of tsutsu and brass tips with openings of various shapes and sizes,
ranging from round and small for medium lines to flat and broad for wide lines. He
selects tsutsu and tip appropriate to the design he will be making. Sixth, Yukiyoshi
or another member of the family who is not busy prepares a batch of rice paste. He
adds water to a mixture of a small amount of lime (calcium hydroxide) and glutinous
rice flour (mochiko) that has been finely ground in a stone mortar (usu). He kneads
the mass into balls. Lime tightens and hardens the paste when it dries. (Some dyers
add rice bran to reduce the mixture's adhesiveness and to make the paste easier to
apply. Bran adds bulk and gives the paste a firm edge capable of resisting dye penetration.) Yukiyoshi boils the balls in water for one hour. He adds water and pounds
the balls into a thick paste. He puts the paste on a small tray or board. He adds a
small amount of water until the paste is just thin enough to flow in the cone. Using
a spatula, Yukiyoshi fills the paper cone with a glob of the paste. (Depending on
the temperature and humidity, salt or more lime may be added to obtain the right
consistency.[14]) Seventh, sitting close to the street windows where the light is good,
Yukiyoshi squeezes a steady flow of rice paste over the lines previously drawn on
the fabric. The work goes at a steady pace. There is no retouching; each line remains
as it was first made. Next, he brushes the surface of the paste with a small brush to
break any air bubbles and he sprinkles rice bran over the paste to prevent sticking and
to hasten drying. He turns the cloth over and, holding it toward the light, applies
paste to the back of the cloth matching exactly the lines on the front.

Eighth, the paste is dried in the sun. Usually Yasushi or his son puts the cloth, still
stretched, at the edge of the street in front of their shop in the bright morning sun-
light. It must dry quickly or the paste will spoil and the design will be ruined. They
dampen the cloth and leave it in the sun to dry again. Ninth, the fabric is painted
twice with gojiru, the liquid extracted from ground soybeans that have been soaked

23. *Nagata Yasushi immersing ceremonial tsutsugaki cotton wrapping cloth in indigo-dye vat. (Nagata dye shop, Izumo. Photo: James R. Brandon)*

24. *Cotton wrapping cloth hanging over indigo vats. Airing promotes oxidation of indigo between immersions. (Nagata dye shop, Izumo. Photo: James R. Brandon)*

25. *Nagata Yasushi wets a cotton tsutsugaki wrapping cloth between dyeings in the Takase River, Izumo. Two furoshiki in different stages of work are drying in front of the shop. (Photo: James R. Brandon)*

26. *Standing in the Takase River, Nagata Shigenobu scrapes rice paste from a finished ceremonial furoshiki decorated with auspicious motifs. (Photo: James R. Brandon)*

in water. The protein in the gojiru undergoes a structural change, known as "denaturation," which renders it insoluble, thus reinforcing the bond between the fibers of cloth and the dye stuff and assuring colorfastness.[15] Nagata wants a deep blue-black dye shade, he mixes pine lampblack and juice extracted from mangrove (*tangara*) into the gojiru before applying it. Nagata does not today use reds or yellow or light greens in the tsutsugaki wrapping cloths he makes, but in the past, if a customer requested them he would paint pigments of these colors on with a brush before dyeing.

Tenth, Nagata takes off the bamboo stretchers and immerses the cloth in dye. The Nagata shop has six vats of indigo dye. After holding the cloth in the dye for three or four minutes, Nagata lifts it out and exposes it to the air for five or six minutes. He repeats this process three or four times. This completes the first dyeing. He and his wife stretch the cloth on bamboo shinshi to wash and dry it once more. At this stage the cloth is a light sky blue color, humorously called *kame nozoki*, "peeking in the vat." To obtain the deep indigo blue hue so prized in Izumo tsutsugaki, Nagata repeats the dyeing process two more times, washing and drying the cloth between each dyeing. If parts of the design are to be kept light blue, he or his brother cover the area with paste from the tsutsu before the second dyeing. When the final dyeing is completed, the piece is thoroughly dried for several days. Complete drying is essential to fix the dyed colors.

Eleventh, the piece is soaked overnight in hot water and the following morning the softened rice paste is washed off. This is usually the job of Nagata's son, Shigenobu, although Nagata may wash important pieces himself. The dyed pieces are then carried across the street to the river. One edge of the fabric is fastened to wooden stakes set in the stream. As the flowing water ripples around the cloth, the rice paste is gently scraped off with an ordinary kitchen spoon, gradually revealing under the water the result of the family's labor. Trucks and cars of a modern age pass by constantly as they work thigh deep in the cold water. Finally, the finished piece is soaked again in hot water, stretched on shinshi, and put in front of the shop to dry one last time.

From the first step to the last, it takes the four members of the Nagata family about twenty days to make one piece. Because dyeing is the trickiest part of the process and can only be done when weather conditions are right, they usually dye ten to twelve pieces at the same time. The Nagata family works hard and continuously. It is often tedious work. But each member of the family shows great pride in the fruits of their labor.

Cotton

The great scholar of Japanese folkways, Yanagida Kunio, once wrote, "when cotton fibers, like white peach blossoms, began floating across our fields, Japan's moonlight was brightened and her nights became more beautiful."[1] The successful cultivation of cotton in Japan between the sixteenth and nineteenth centuries indeed brought new light to Japanese agriculture, revolutionizing rural life commercially in many parts of the country and altering village life style everywhere. The arrival of cotton, as Yanagida imaginatively suggests, marked the beginning of a new era in the modest world of the commoner. And it was the ready supply of locally grown cotton that made the development of tsutsugaki-textile culture possible in the countryside.

Since early times an unwritten law held that silk clothing—used in Japan since the third century—was reserved for the aristocracy, the priestly class, and samurai. Numerous government edicts during the Edo period expressly forbade commoners to wear fine silk garments. These rules were directed primarily at urban commoners (rich merchants and Kabuki actors, for example) who had the money to buy silk clothes, not at poor farmers and villagers who couldn't afford silk in any event. Nor did people in the country wear cotton clothes before the sixteenth century. Cotton fabrics had been imported from China for aristocratic use for perhaps a thousand years (the earliest cotton fabric preserved in Japan at the Hōryūji is attributed to the 7th century).[2] But they were rare and expensive.

Before the advent of cotton planting in Japan, fabrics that were available to common people and especially those living in the countryside were made of coarse fibers such as hemp, arrowroot, wisteria, Japanese linden, or paper mulberry. Fibers obtained from these plant stems and tree barks were strong and durable, but they required tedious hours of labor to produce, and the coarse fabrics made from them were uncomfortable against the skin and inefficient insulators. Several layers of clothing had to be worn during the winter. A common way of describing a particularly cold season was to call it "a winter of two layers" or "a winter of three layers."

Considerable quantities of Korean and Chinese cotton fabrics were imported into Japan during the fourteenth and fifteenth centuries, but until Japanese farmers grew cotton themselves, clothes made of this wonderful fabric remained out of their reach.[3] The *Chronology of Japanese History* (*Nihon kōki*; 840), a forty-volume imperial compilation edited by Fujiwara Fuyutsugu, Fujiwara Morotsugu, and other court officials, describes in Volume Eight the initial introduction of cotton cultivation. A young man, speaking Chinese and possibly from a country in Southeast Asia, drifted ashore in a small boat in the summer of 799. He sang, played a stringed instrument, and brought with him cotton seeds.[4] The *General Encyclopedia of National History* (*Ruijū kokushi*; 893), two hundred volumes, compiled by the court scholar Sugawara Michizane, tells how the seeds were washed, soaked overnight, and planted in warm earth four per hole in various parts of the country.[5] Unfortunately, the seeds did not grow, probably because the species was not suited to Japan's climate.[6] In the sixteenth century a species of cotton long cultivated in China and Korea, and probably originating in the Indus River civilization, was successfully introduced into Japan.[7] It flourished in Japan's soil and climate, especially in the central and western parts of the country. A shrine document of the period 1504–20 mentions early cotton cultivation in Mikawa (present Aichi Prefecture) and the selling of cotton at a market in Nara. Numerous other records attest to widespread cultivation in the sixteenth century.[8] Writing in 1696, Miyazaki Yasusada described major cotton-growing areas as the fertile plain around Osaka consisting of Kawachi, Settsu, and Izumi districts as well as high-quality land formerly used for grain cultivation in Harima (west of Osaka) and Bingo (Hiroshima Prefecture).[9] Other noted producing areas were Owari, Yamato-Koriyama, Musashi, Omi, Ise, Mino, Hida, Tamba, and Tajima. Only in the north was the weather too severe for cotton plants to grow. The finest cotton was reputed to come from Isematsuzaka (Gifu Prefecture) and Kawachi.[10]

At first farmers grew cotton for personal use. Women raised cotton on a part of their land and they ginned, spun, wove, and dyed it in their homes to clothe their families. Because making cotton textiles was nearly a self-sufficient operation, when cotton began to be grown, common people were able to clothe themselves in this new material and create tsutsugaki momen for ceremonial use. In the seventeenth century, cotton clothing rapidly increased in popularity, both in the cities and the countryside, and in response to this demand farmers were able to sell cotton as a cash crop. Some farmers carried out the whole process from cultivation to weaving, some specialized in cultivation only, and some cultivated and sold ginned cotton to others to spin or to weave. In villages, some became specialist weavers. Lured by the prospect of profit, men became spinners and weavers, work formerly reserved for women.[11] Raw cotton, processed cotton, and finished-cotton fabrics were bought by middlemen and sold to wholesalers in Osaka, who redistributed the cotton goods to villages and towns in distant places. By the mid-Edo period, cotton-textile trade was contributing more than half of all the rural income in major cotton-producing areas.[12] Trade in cotton introduced a powerful money economy into rural life. The involvement of villagers in that trade was an important factor linking the Japanese countryside to the broad cash-marketing system of the nation, preparing the way for Japan's rapid modernization in the Meiji era.

In parts of Japan farmers converted the majority of rice land to cotton growing in order to maximize their cash income.[13] Government edicts lectured against the practice to little avail. Unquestionably it was risky economics. If the weather was good and cotton prices were high, a farmer could become wealthy—the novelist Ihara Saikaku vividly describes how one destitute farmer named Kusuke made a fortune selling cotton fluffed with a device he invented.[14] But cotton is a weather-sensitive crop and its price fluctuated widely. If the crop was bad and prices low, small landowners who had put fifty or seventy-five percent of their rice land into cotton might be forced to sell their family land and become tenant cultivators of larger, richer landowners. Cotton and cotton textiles contributed to loosening rural social structure and wealth increasingly determined social status in the countryside long before the modern era in Japan.

While the cotton-growing regions were entering into a new era, where cotton did not grow the old system of home weaving for home use continued. In Tohoku, northern Japan, hemp was the major fiber that was woven as late as the mid-Meiji era. Women in Aichi-Furikusa Village, for example, cultivated hemp and wove it into cloth which they exchanged for ginned cotton. They then spun and wove the cotton into cloth to make garments for their family members. This practice was known as "bartered cotton" (torikae momen).[15] Even after machine-made cotton took over the Japanese cotton industry in the late nineteenth century, village cotton weaving continued in many remote areas. Up through the 1890s many farm women wove all the clothing that their families wore. In Tohoku the word momen (cotton) often meant luxurious cloth.

Today we take cotton for granted but to commoners in sixteenth-century Japan the qualities of the new fiber were exceptional. Cotton was soft, warm, and comfortable to wear. It was pliable and could be woven into many kinds of fabrics. Unspun cotton wadding proved ideal for stuffing winter garments or mattresses (in fact commoners had never slept on mattresses before the advent of cotton). Cotton was relatively easy to process, from harvesting through ginning and spinning to weaving. Work clothes made of cotton were strong and durable. Cotton took some natural dyes better than hemp or other coarse fibers (but not as well as silk). Indigo dye in particular produced beautiful, rich blues on cotton.

The species of cotton plant cultivated in Japan from the sixteenth century is believed to have been *Gossypium arboreum*, race *sinense*, one of a score of plants of the mallow (*Malvaceae*) family that provide cotton fibers in various parts of the world. Cotton plants in Japan grow two to three feet tall. Five-petaled flowers—yellow, white, and later in the season pink or red—bloom during summer and fall, producing seedpods the size of an egg. A pod's three or four sections each contain five to seven seeds. It is the hairs of these seeds, at first tightly packed within their bolls, that burst open on maturity as a soft mass of white fibers. Farmers in Japan planted in May and picked in September. The bolls were dried for two or three days and then crushed between rollers of a hand-cranked ginning machine (*rokuro*) to remove the inch-long cotton fibers from the seeds. In a separate process, the seeds were pressed to make cottonseed oil. Fibers were separated by an unusual device called *wata uchiyumi* (cotton-striking bow). It consisted of a cord (*tsuru*) stretched taut by an arced wooden

27. *A machine for crushing cotton balls, based on a woodblock print, "Harvesting Cotton in Kawachi," published in* Illustrations of Japanese Products (Dainippon bussan zukai), *late 19th century. (Drawing: Dan Liu)*

28. *A cotton-fluffing bow* (watauchiyumi), *based on an illustration in the 18th-century* Poems of One Hundred Artisans (Imayō shokunin zukushi hyakunin isshu). *(Drawing: Dan Liu)*

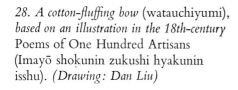

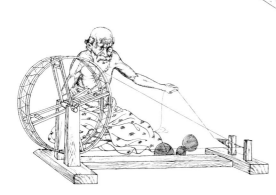

29. *A spinning wheel* (itoguruma) *used for spinning cotton thread, based on an illustration in Ōkura Nagatsune's* Basic Facts About Cotton (Menpo yōmu), *1833. (Drawing: Dan Liu)*

bow (*yumi*). Struck with a small mallet, the vibrating cord snapped fibers out of the cotton mass, fluffing them and separating them in the process. This work required considerable skill; increasingly during the Edo period it was done by specialists (*wata uchiya*, cotton strikers) who traveled from village to village, hiring themselves out. The fluffed cotton then was spread flat, rolled into small tubes (*shinomaki*) by hand, and spun into thread on a spinning wheel to ready for weaving.[16]

Plain-weave cotton is the most usual fabric used for making country tsutsugaki. In farm homes the cloth was usually woven on a back-strap loom, the izaribata or sitting loom.[17] This type of loom has been used in Japan since the fifth century.[18] In most parts of Japan the basic design of izaribata is the same, although details may vary. The izaribata is a simple loom. A wooden frame supports a back beam holding

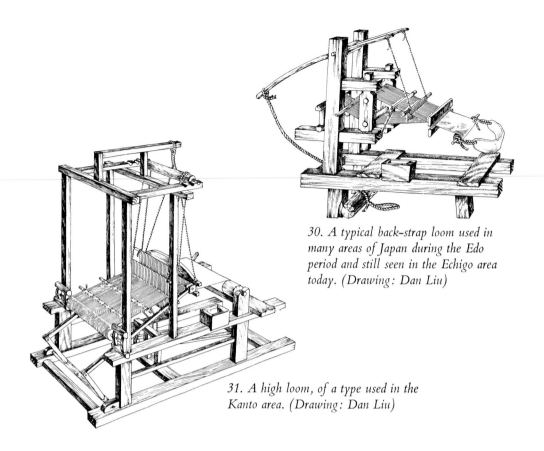

30. A typical back-strap loom used in many areas of Japan during the Edo period and still seen in the Echigo area today. (Drawing: Dan Liu)

31. A high loom, of a type used in the Kanto area. (Drawing: Dan Liu)

the warp, a front beam attached to the body of the weaver by a strap (back strap), and a single set of heddles controlled by pulling a cord with one foot. The most significant feature of the loom is that the weaver moves his or her body forward or backward to regulate the amount of tension on the warp threads stretched between the back beam and the weaver's body. An advantage of the loom is that the weaver can easily loosen the warps to accommodate hand-spun threads of irregular size or coarse fibers such as hemp which do not stretch. A disadvantage is that changes in warp tension caused by the weaver's body movements can produce an irregular weave. This primitive loom depended on the human qualities of the person weaving and in each piece of plain-weave cotton fabric woven on it the personal touch of that weaver is noticeable. The special qualities of ceremonial tsutsugaki momen, especially early pieces, are inseparable from the hand-spun and hand-woven cotton that was born on this variable, human-scale loom.

By the nineteenth century, cotton cloth was also being hand woven on more sophisticated horizontal looms called *takahata* (high loom). Takahata were originally used for silk weaving. They have rigid frames to hold the warps and two sets of counterbalanced heddles. The warps, attached to opposing beams, are stretched mechanically at constant tension throughout weaving so that these looms produce cotton cloth of great consistency. Takahata came to be used in many villages but izaribata also continued to exist, producing unique hand-woven cotton textiles.

Indigo

When cotton was widely available to Japanese commoners in the seventeenth century, it became a great adventure to dye the new fabric with indigo, perhaps the favorite color in rural Japan. When cotton cloth was dipped into indigo, the result proved to be remarkably beautiful. On cotton cloth, the indigo produced a lustrous shade of deep blue. Not only did cotton take indigo dye extremely well, it was discovered that repeated dippings built up layers of indigo dye around the cotton fibers, rendering them extremely durable. The medicinal properties of indigo were recorded in China as early as the Han dynasty (A.D. 25–220). In China and Japan indigo leaves and seeds were used to treat insect and snake bites, fever, and stomach disorders, and materials dyed in indigo were considered efficacious as well. Throughout Japan farmers believed that work clothes dyed in indigo would protect them from snakes in the field. The natural ammonia in indigo was believed to act as an antivenin. It was also believed that the distinctive odor of indigo-dyed cloth drove snakes away.[1] Indigo's dark color served to hide stains and dirt that soiled a working man's clothes. In some areas, when soap was not easily available, stained cloth was dyed in indigo instead of being washed. Cotton was soft and absorbent and was comfortable to wear during strenuous work. From both practical and aesthetic points of view, the new *aizome momen,* or indigo-dyed cotton, proved to be the ideal type of fabric for commoners' daily use. The bent figures of farmers, dressed in deep indigo-blue cotton jacket and trousers, silhouetted against green rice fields, became a typical scene in Japanese rural life. In time, the term aizome momen came to be used symbolically to indicate the basic textile culture of the common people in Japan.

Indigo (*ai*) is the general term given to a group of plants that contain indican, a water-soluble colorless substance that turns a blue, or indigo, color when it oxidizes as a result of exposure to the air. The origins of Japanese indigo-dye making go back to ancient times. The most primitive method of coloring fabric blue was rubbing leaves of wild mountain indigo (*yama ai*) directly onto cloth. Yama ai (*Mercurialis*

32. Indigo plants growing in Awa, Toku-shima, before harvest. (Photo: Barbara Stephan)

leiocarpa Sieb. et Zucc.) grows wild in shady and forested land. It is not, strictly speaking, an indigo plant, for its leaves do not contain indican: chlorophyll in the leaves makes a light blue-green dye. In ancient times, mountain indigo was a sacred dye and was used to color the special purified garments worn by the emperor on the occasion of his enthronement.[2] The *Records of Ancient Matters* (*Kojiki;* 712) and the poetry anthology *Ten Thousand Leaves* (*Man'yōshū;* 8th century) refer to this method of dyeing.[3] Rubbing leaves on cloth was an inefficient method of coloring, for the dye did not penetrate the fibers but only weakly colored the surface. The deep blue indigo colors for which Japanese country textiles are famous come from the leaves of the *tade ai* plant (a buckwheat, *Polygonum tinctorium* Lour.), which was introduced to Japan from China in the fifth and sixth centuries. Tade ai was domesticated by the Nara period and the sight of its bright green leaves, and tiny red and white blossoms, was soon common throughout the country.

Indigo-dye baths can be prepared in a number of ways.[4] Dyeing with fresh indigo leaves (*nama ha zome*) was a simple method of indigo dyeing known in the Nara and Heian periods. Freshly gathered leaves were crushed and mixed with water to produce a dye bath. The indican (also called white indigo) in the water would affix to an immersed fabric and the fabric would become blue after exposure to air. Even today dyeing is sometimes done with fresh leaves but it is not a practical way to do large-scale or continuous dyeing. A dye bath made of fresh leaves can only be used a short time. A further disadvantage is that fresh leaves cannot be gathered throughout the year.

Fermented dye baths represent the next significant change in dyeing techniques. Fermentation removes the oxygen from the indigo-dye bath, thereby converting previously oxidized and insoluble indigo (or indigotin) back into soluble indican. Fermentation inhibits oxidation in the dye bath, thereby extending the time the bath can be used for dyeing. A dye bath made of fresh leaves can naturally ferment in the heat of summer. Today in Okinawa fresh leaves of Okinawan indigo, a variety of indigofera, are often fermented naturally to make a dye bath. It was also discovered that indigo dye could be produced by fermenting dried leaves of the indigo plant. *Codes of the Engi Era (Engishiki)*, a court compilation of 924, gives significant details of dyeing of that time. It lists dyes, mordants, and other materials used for each major dye color. To obtain blue dye dry indigo leaves and ash lye are listed as necessary ingredients (indicating fermentation) and it also states that indigo dyeing is done between July 1 and September 30.[5]

A more advanced method of fermentation was probably developed by the Muromachi period. Dry indigo leaves were composted in an enclosed space and made into a concentrate (*sukumo*) which was again fermented in a large ceramic vat to make a dye bath. A great advantage of sukumo was that it could be transported to distant places. It made a concentrated dye bath that shortened dyeing time while producing an intense deep blue color. Several conditions were necessary to keep the fermentation process going: an alkaline pH level between ten and eleven; a vat temperature of twenty-five to thirty-five degrees celsius; and a supply of nutrients to feed the bacterial process. A final development, enclosing the ceramic jars in pits and heating the dye baths, made it possible to dye cloth in winter months as well as summer. Pit heating may have begun in the Kamakura period and it seems to have been established by the Muromachi period. This method of preparing indigo from sukumo in a fermenting, artificially heated dye bath came to be called "true indigo dyeing" (*shōaizome*) and became very widespread in the making of country tsutsugaki momen.

Through most of early Japanese history, village women grew their own indigo plants, prepared their own dyestuff, and dyed their family's clothing themselves. The classic term for indigo dyeing, *konkaki* (indigo stirring), has a homey flavor. The tradition of women dyeing at home continued in remote areas into the twentieth century. However, in general, indigo dyeing shifted into the hands of professional dyers. This transition seems to have begun in the twelfth century. Women appear as professional indigo dyers in paintings of the Muromachi period. In a typical scene drawn by Tosa Mitsunobu (1434–1525) in *Seventy-one Illustrated Songs (Shichijūichiban utaawase)*, a woman is bent over a huge free-standing dye vat, swirling a cloth in the dye bath.[6] A famous screen painting by Kanō Yoshinobu (1552–1640), the *Kita Temple Artisans Screen (Kitain shokunin zukushi byōbu)*, shows a woman dyeing a cloth in a dye vat half-sunk into a pit. This suggests fermentation dyeing and protection of the vat to contain its heat.[7] As indigo-dyed cotton cloth became increasingly popular in the Edo period, indigo dyeing became an independent profession for male artisans who established commercial dye shops in cities and villages. The change is shown in a picture in *The New Style Pattern Book (Shingata komonchō; 1824)*, in which a male dyer carries in each dripping hand indigo-dyed cloths held flat on stretchers. Beside the sunken vats is a hole for tending the fire that keeps the fermentation process going continuously.[8]

In the late sixteenth century, Toyotomi Hideyoshi promulgated a fundamental law that separated the classes in terms of occupation and place of residence. Commercial artisans, such as the male dyers just mentioned, were forced to reside and work in cities and they were not allowed to farm. In the city they were subject to strict control

33. Above left: *a dyeing scene from the early 16th century, showing a woman bent over a free-standing dye vat, based on an illustration in* Seventy-One Illustrated Songs (Shichi-jūichiban utaawase). *(Drawing: Dan Liu)*

34. Above: *a woman dyeing in a half-sunken dye vat, based on the screen,* Kita Temple Artisans (Kitain shokunin zukushi byōbu), *of the late 16th or early 17th century. (Drawing: Dan Liu)*

35. *A professional male dyer of the 19th century, based on an illustration in the* New Style Pattern Book (Shingata komonchō). *(Drawing: Dan Liu)*

and taxation; a government revenue agent (*kon'ya gashira,* indigo-dyers' head) levied a tax payable in money or dyed fabrics on each indigo vat an artisan owned.[9] A farmer, on the other hand, was commanded to live on his land and engage only in farming. He was forbidden to undertake any commercial enterprise, such as making dyed goods and selling them to others. In theory people were not allowed to move from one occupational group to another.

In practice, however, concurrent with the rapid development of a money economy in the nation during the Edo period, such distinctions broke down. Dye artisans moved out of the large cities into small towns and villages where they set up shops to meet the rural demand for indigo-dyed cotton fabric. And farmers opened dye shops while still cultivating their fields.[10] Typically these were family enterprises employing a few local workers. Commercial village dye shops were of two common kinds: front dye houses (*omote kon'ya*), which specialized in dyeing tsutsugaki or kata-zome fabrics, and thread dye houses (*ito kon'ya*), which dyed threads for weavers prior to weaving. Some shops handled both types of dyeing. Indigo preparation and dyeing required sophisticated knowledge. Farm women who in earlier times dyed for themselves increasingly turned to village dye shops, perhaps due to indigo dyeing's inherent complexity. It was common in the Edo period for women to bring their skeins of cotton thread to the local dyeing shop: following this custom tsutsugaki dyeing also was done by professionals.

Some idea of the numbers of dye artisans involved can be gleaned from local records. In the town of Shimabara in Nagasaki Prefecture in 1707, dyers were the most numerous of the various artisans. Out of a total 1,213 houses there were 115 artisans' shops of fourteen kinds (carpenters, coopers, mat makers, tool sharpeners, sword-handle makers, lacquerware artisans, wood carvers, blacksmiths, roofers, etc.). The highest number of these, 30, were dye shops.[11] The register of the provincial city of Kofu, Yamanashi Prefecture for the period 1804–17 lists 67 dye shops among a total of 344 artisan shops of fifteen trades. The number of dyers exceeds all other trades.[12] Even a country village like Mugikura, Saitama Prefecture, with a population of 1,726, boasted 6 dye shops.[13]

Most professional artisan-dyers did not grow indigo themselves; they purchased sukumo from areas specializing in indigo cultivation. Important centers of sukumo production were Sanuki and Iyo (Kagawa Prefecture), Mino (Gifu Prefecture), Settsu (Hyogo Prefecture), Bizen (Okayama Prefecture), and Chikugo (Saga Prefecture). The best sukumo was said to come from indigo grown in Awa, Tokushima Pre-fecture, Shikoku Island, where fertile conditions were assured by the yearly flood-ing of the Yoshino River plain. Indigo was first grown in Awa in the early seventeenth century and production peaked around 1902. Awa indigo (*awa ai*) was so highly prized that production methods were kept secret and selling indigo leaves or seeds outside the area was prohibited to protect the industry. Especially in the mid–eight-eenth century this prohibition was strictly enforced, and it is recorded that some Awa farmers who broke the rules were beheaded.[14]

Today, four indigo-compost producers in Tokushima continue the old traditions of making indigo sukumo. The Satō family, whose indigo farm is located on the north side of the Yoshino River, is the largest of these. The Satō family grows indigo

36. *Spreading harvested indigo leaves to dry, prior to making concentrate. (Satō Akito indigo farm, Tokushima. Photo: Alex Anderson)*

37. *Indigo compost on clay bed in Tokushima. (Satō Akito indigo farm, Tokushima. Photo: Barbara Stephan)*

on about one hectare of land and they purchase leaves from another four hectares of indigo plants grown by neighboring farmers. In one year they produce about two hundred fifty bags of sukumo compost (a bag is 56 kilograms). Dyers and artists throughout the country buy up the family's sukumo because of its high quality.

Indigo seeds are planted in beds in February or early March—at the time the swallows return to Tokushima, according to Satō Akito, who is the third-generation head of the family firm. In May the five- to six-inch seedlings are transplanted by hand to dry fields. The top of the plant is harvested in June–July and a second growth of leaves in August. The plants are dried and chopped and the leaves are winnowed from the stems using electric fans (wind in previous times). At this point sukumo making begins. On an astrologically auspicious day in September, according to the

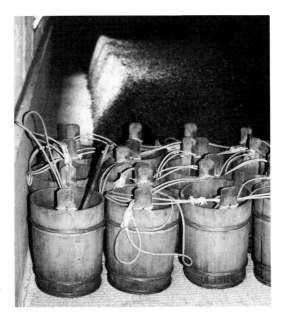

38. *Buckets for watering indigo compost pile. (Satō Akito indigo farm, Tokushima. Photo: Alex Anderson)*

old calendar, Satō's workers pile the harvested leaves (up to 4 tons) a meter deep on specially prepared compost beds made of successive layers of gravel, sand, chaff, sand, and clay. The leaves are thoroughly dampened. The material of the bed retains any runoff water and returns it through evaporation thus helping to maintain proper humidity. Every five or six days Satō and his workers splash the leaves with buckets of water and aerate them by raking and turning. This is done twenty or more times (Satō keeps track of the number with chalk marks on a pole beside the compost bed at each watering). By around the twelfth watering, the composting mass forms into hard clumps that Satō and his men break apart by raking and sifting the compost through a broad mesh screen. By the seventeenth or eighteenth watering, the hardening compost is sifted again. (In the Edo period, a third sifting was done as well.)

As the weather in October grows colder, Satō covers over the piles of leaves with thick straw mats to retain the heat of the composting mass. The mats are tied down with ropes (in the past they were also weighted with stones weighing 3 to 4 tons). The heat that is generated is so intense steam rises from the leaves. High quality sukumo is produced only when the temperature of the compost (55–60 degrees C) and its wetness are in proper balance. At the end of composting, the sukumo is one-twentieth the volume and sixty-five percent of the weight of the original leaves. During the Edo period, highly respected professionals known as water specialists (*mizushi*) were contracted to travel a circuit from one indigo plantation to the next to check the moisture and temperature of sukumo beds. When one came to a compost bed, he sensed how much water was needed by the smell of the indigo and the amount of heat rising from the indigo pile. After about one hundred days the completed sukumo compost is packed into straw bags for distribution.[15]

Traditional indigo growers and dyers hold special views of their profession.

39. *Offering of a cedar sprig in sake bottle—a prayer for success in sukumo making. (Satō Akito indigo farm, Tokushima. Photo: Alex Anderson)*

Success is not directly attributed to their own ability but rather to proper dedication to the needs of the task, personal humility, and the beneficence of the deities. It was mid-September when I visited the Satō farm and indigo leaves were already heaped onto beds that filled three farm buildings. Composting was under way—the leaves were so hot you could not touch them with your bare hand. On each mound of leaves a small branch in a sake bottle had been placed to honor the guardian deity of dyers and to pray for successful sukumo making. According to Satō, when he feels unhappy, the indigo mirrors his unhappiness and the result of the day's work is not good.

During the Edo period sukumo was also dried, pounded, and pressed into concentrated pellets (*aidama*) for easy transport to distant parts of the country. (Today, instead of making pellets, dried sukumo is pressed into blocks by machine.) An expert can judge the elasticity, texture, and color of sukumo or aidama by mixing a bit of the indigo with water in the palm of the hand and then pressing the palm against handmade paper.[16]

It requires skill and patience to make an indigo-dye bath from sukumo or aidama in the traditional manner. Details of the process vary from place to place and from artisan to artisan and in the past were closely guarded secrets. The same basic steps in the process, however, are practiced by many traditional dyers in Japan, including the Nagatas in Izumo, who purchase their sukumo from the Awa region of

40. *Nagata Yasushi stirring fermenting indigo in dye vat. (Nagata dye shop, Izumo. Photo: James R. Brandon)*

41. *Dipping tsutsugaki cotton into indigo dye vat. Fermentation bubbles,* ai no hana, *cover the surface. (Ōkawahara dye shop, Takamatsu. Photo: Barbara Stephan)*

Tokushima. The appropriate quantity of sukumo or aidama is kneaded in a mortar with ash-lye water (*haijiru*)—water that has been strained through wood ash. The resulting soft indigo paste is placed in a large vat. Ash water sufficient to fill the vat four-fifths full is added along with lime (*sekkai*). Bacteria begin converting sukumo into soluble indican within a few days (concentrated mixtures start fermenting sooner than weak mixtures). The traditional dyer tastes and smells the mixture daily to check the state of fermentation. For fermentation to continue an appropriate level of alkalinity must be maintained (pH 10–11). This is done by adding more lime, an alkali, usually two or more times. Nutrients such as rice wine, honey, or rice bran are added to feed the bacteria. The temperature of the vat must be kept between twenty-five and thirty-five degrees celsius, either naturally or with artificial heat. Each day the dye bath is gently stirred to equalize temperature and pH level throughout the mixture (too-vigorous stirring will introduce oxygen, which halts the fermentation process). Golden-purple fermentation bubbles called "indigo flowers" (*ai no hana*) collect on the surface of the dye bath, usually after four to seven days. Dyers say the "indigo is blooming," and dyeing can begin.

Traditional dye workers treat a dye bath as something individual, with a personality and a life of its own. Shinto respect and reverence for the life in nature lives in the indigo dyer's dark workroom. A dyer feeds the bath to please it and to make it docile, as he would a person. A dyer who is concerned about the slow rate of fer-

42. Miniature paper kimono, dyed indigo on the bottom, presented as an offering to the deities at the time of the first dyeing of the New Year (hatsuzome). *(Photo: Shufunotomo)*

mentation asks the indigo to "behave." The dye bath is as much a part of nature as is the dyer. For some dyers, indigo vats are sacred places where a protective deity dwells; they make offerings at the beginning of each year to please the deity. The guardian deity of dyers is Aizen Myōō (Rāga-rāja), whose name means "dyed in love." Fierce on the outside and compassionate in his heart, Aizen Myōō is an esoteric deity of the Shingon sect of Buddhism. He was probably adopted by dyers as their deity because "ai" also means indigo.[17] As part of the New Year's ritual a miniature kimono, cut from handmade paper and partially dipped in indigo dye, was traditionally offered to the deity's shrine in the dyer's shop. The dyed kimono symbolizes a request for good fortune during the coming year.

Future

Can traditional tsutsugaki artisans continue to work and survive in Japan's highly technological economy today? Can their craft have a function in contemporary society? Certainly no Japanese textile craftsman or craftswoman is untouched by modern life.

Many dyers continue to hold a basically traditional attitude toward their craft and profession, accepting an essential spiritual relationship between themselves and their work. They accept, as did tsutsugaki artisans of the Edo period, the necessity for hardship, dedication, patience, concentration, repetition, and experience without expecting the result to be wholly under their control.

Traditional tsutsugaki dyeing—drawing freehand designs in rice paste and dip-dyeing—survives today only under special circumstances. Nagata Yasushi and his family continue to make ceremonial furoshiki in Izumo with a few adjustments to modern times. Sometimes the cloth is not hand woven and they receive no orders for yogi or futonji. But he follows craft techniques that he learned from his father and that he is passing on to his son. He maintains the traditional motifs and methods of working. He does not produce modern designs to appeal to a mass market. His customers are mostly local people. Although he is now nationally known—his craft has been named an Important Cultural Property of Shimane Prefecture and he has received magazine and television publicity—anyone who visits his somber dyeing room will sense the stability of his life and work. Six buried indigo dye vats show their open tops. Light occasionally hits the surface of brown-blue liquid that fills each vat to the brim. Dark tsutsugaki fabrics, in various stages of dyeing, are the proper products of this traditional life. Nagata and his son carry the tradition into the future more or less intact.

Tsutsugaki also survives in Takamatsu, a port city on the north coast of Shikoku Island, in more modernized form. Ōkawahara Shizuo, a sixth-generation indigo dyer, runs a successful dye shop on a bustling commercial street of the city. The inner

43. *Finished tsutsugaki banners drying in the sun. (Ōkawahara dye shop, Takamatsu. Photo: Barbara Stephan)*

courtyard of his house and shop gives a dazzling display of criss-crossing dyed banners and other textiles. Strong motifs and ideographs are painted, printed, and dyed on dozens of long strips of cloth hung on stretchers and drying in midair. Ōkawahara and his assistants draw and dye in genuine tsutsugaki technique shop curtains which boast the merchants' special logos, brilliant pennants that will fly over fishing boats, and colorful Lion Dance (*shishi mai*) costumes and banners for local shrine festivals. He keeps four vats of true indigo in his dye shop, but he uses indigo only for special pieces. He makes an excellent livelihood filling textile orders for the people who live in his city and the neighboring villages. They want bright colors—and that means chemical dyes—and reasonable prices—which means he uses machine-made fabrics. Hand dyeing is still strongly related to the seasons and special festivals. When the sound of practice drumming is heard in Takamatsu, Ōkawahara's dye shop becomes extremely busy meeting new orders for banners and Lion Dance costumes for the coming festival. There are no orders today for ceremonial wedding futonji or a delicate phoenix design. Ōkawahara's mother cherishes the dim memory of seeing indigo-dyed phoenix, crane, and tortoise on ceremonial futon covers; yet it's no longer possible to live by doing true indigo dyeing. Ōkawahara is an excellent tsutsugaki craftsman who was trained by his father. He thinks he could make indigo phoenixes and lions as good as his grandfather's if a generous customer gave him the chance.

Plates

1. *Yogi*

2. *Yogi*

7. *Futonji*

9. *Futonji*

10. *Futonji*

11. *Futonji*

17. *Futonji,* probably altered from *yogi*

19. *Futonji*

3. Yogi

4. *Yogi*

5. *Yogi*

6. *Futonji*

8. *Futonji*

12. *Futonji*, altered from *yogi*

13. *Futonji*

4

14. *Futonji*, altered from *yogi*

72 • PLATES

15. *Futonji*, probably altered from *yogi*

16. *Futonji*, probably altered from *yogi*

18. *Futonji*, probably altered from *yogi*

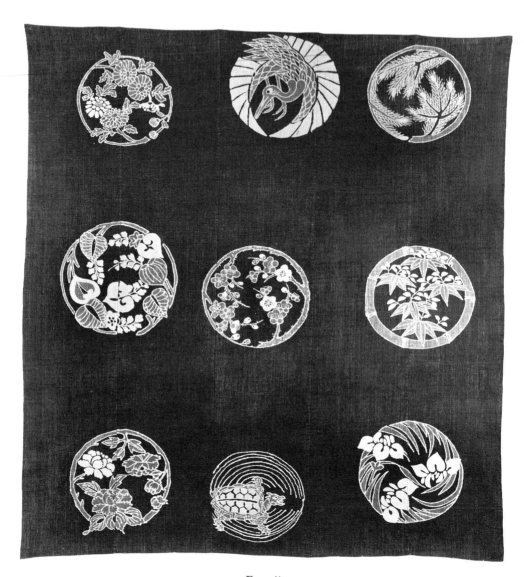

20. *Futonji*

21. *Futonji*

22. *Futonji*

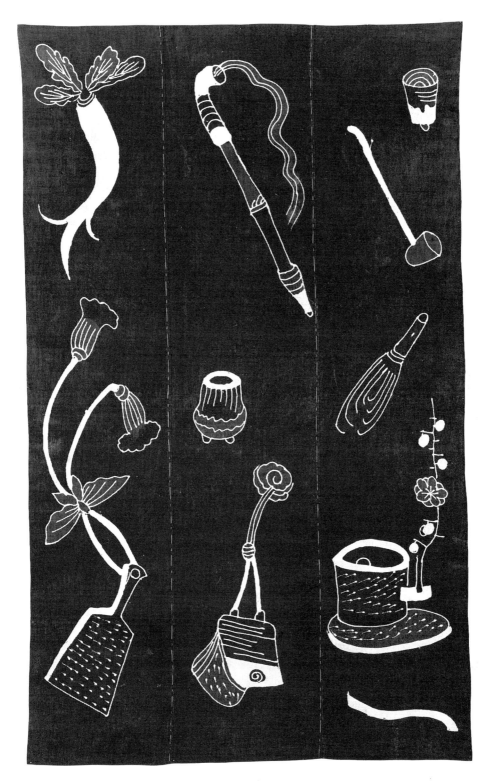

23. *Futonji*

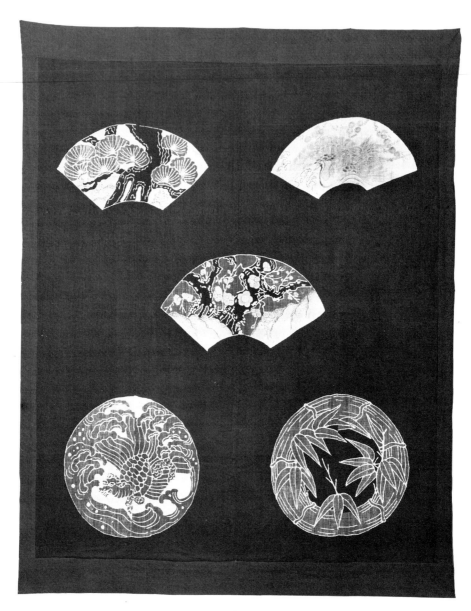

24. *Futonji*

31. *Furoshiki* or *Yutan*

32. *Furoshiki*

35. *Furoshiki*

36. *Furoshiki*

44. *Maiwai*

45. *Kazuki* or *Katsugi*

46. *Noren*

48. Hanging made from a jacket

25. Futonji

26. *Futonji*

27. *Futonji*

28. *Yutan* or *Furoshiki*

29. *Yutan* or *Noren*

30. *Furoshiki*

33. *Furoshiki*

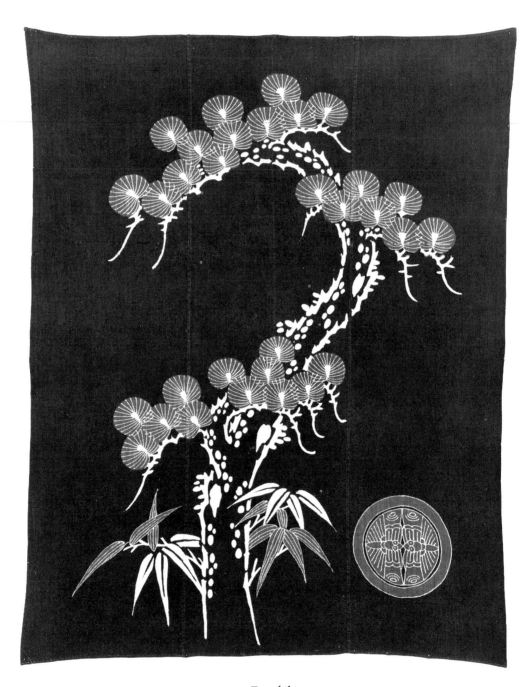

34. *Furoshiki*

37. *Furoshiki*

38. *Yuage*

39. Ceremonial cloth

40. *Kooi*

41. *Kooi*

42. Portion of a girl's kimono

43. *Nobori*

47. *Noren*

Commentaries on the Plates

1. *Yogi* (p. 57)

Saga Prefecture, Kyushu Island, mid-19th century

Cotton, hand spun, hand woven, plain weave, rice-paste resist, painted
   with pigments, dip-dyed in indigo

Pale shades of blue, pink, brown, orange, and yellow on deep blue

Kimono construction with extra central panel; 12″ panel

l. (hem to neck) 62″ (157 cm.); collar 5″ (13 cm.); w. (sleeve to sleeve)
   62½″ (158 cm.)

Honolulu Academy of Arts, gift of Eleanor Burts, in memory of Alex-
   andra Coffman, 1985 (#5364.1)

This exceptionally beautiful yogi was preserved as an heirloom by a
wealthy family from Saga, northern Kyushu. It has been reconstructed
with original lining which extends, traditionally as it seems here, both
sleeve openings, the hem line, and collar ends, giving the piece spacious-
ness as a sleeping cover. The motif is the familiar *shōchikubai*, containing
the longevity symbols of the "three friends of the cold season." The
lively yet careful execution of the three trees—dramatically straight bamboo and parallel, curving plum and pine growing upward—and the
subtle coloring of the pigments testify to the exceptional skill of the
tsutsugaki craftsman who created this sophisticated yogi. Unusual in
country tsutsugaki dyeing is the careful, painterly rendering of the texture
of the pine tree in pale brown and grey pigments. In contrast, the trunk
of the plum tree is suggested with a few strong white tsutsugaki strokes.
Clusters of pine needles, bamboo leaves, and plum blossoms are finely
detailed in narrow white tsutsugaki lines. At the same time, subtle shading on the leaves and blossoms (from pale greens to blues, from light blue
to grey, and pink to grey to white) creates a delicate effect that provides
a pleasing balance to the boldness of the overall design.

2. *Yogi* (p. 58)

Fukuoka Prefecture, late 19th century

Cotton, hand spun, hand woven, plain weave, rice-paste resist, painted
  with pigments, dip-dyed in indigo

Natural white, tangerine, grey, moss green, and light blue on dark
  indigo blue

Kimono construction with gussets; 13½″ panel

l. (hem to neck) 55½″ (141 cm.); collar 3″ (7 cm.); w. (sleeve to sleeve)
  51½″ (131 cm.)

Honolulu Academy of Arts, purchase, 1985 (#5333.1)

Three separate sets of gay shōchikubai motifs grow upward from the
hem. The large central shōchikubai pattern fills the two wide back panels
and the topmost branches spread out into both sleeves. One of the
interesting decorative conventions of this motif is that pine-needle clusters, bamboo leaves, and plum blossoms all grow out of a single twisting
plum or pine tree that forms the center core. An illusion is created that
a single tree gives birth to the three plants. This particular shōchikubai has
affinities with the standing-tree motif (*tachiki mon'yō*) of Edo-era kosode,
which in turn was influenced by the Tree of Life pattern seen on the
batik chintzes that were imported into Japan from India at that time. In
the upper center, above the tree, there is a large *mokkō* (melon) crest,
enclosed in a ring of wisteria blossoms (*fujiwa*), in light indigo blue (a
shade produced in the early stage of dyeing). The melon is a popular
family crest of Chinese origin and wisteria was once the powerful Fujiwara clan's crest. This may be a single family crest, or the wisteria may
be a purely decorative addition to the melon crest (a ring of wisteria often
is a festive decoration) or represent the crests of the bride's and groom's
families combined. The white lines bordering the inner parts of the crest
are not perfectly drawn (as they usually are), which suggests a casual,
country flavor. Otherwise, this is an elegant wedding yogi that is in
excellent condition. The bright red pigment is extremely well preserved,
giving this kimono cover a warm, lively touch.

3. *Yogi* (p. 65)

Northern Kyushu, Meiji period (1868–1912)

Cotton, hand spun, hand woven, plain weave, rice-paste resist, painted
  with pigments, dip-dyed in indigo

Natural white, pale shades of brown, moss green, lavender, grey, and
  pink on indigo blue

Kimono construction with extra central panel and gussets; 12½″ panel

l. (hem to neck) 52″ (132 cm.); collar 2½″ (6 cm.); w. (sleeve to sleeve)
  56½″ (143 cm.)

Honolulu Academy of Arts, purchase, 1985 (#5332.1)

A large flying crane, in lovely pale shades of brown, green, lavender, and
grey, descending from the shoulder and extending its wings across both
sleeves, dominates this unusual yogi. Anchoring the bold pattern and

giving it balance are an auspicious "tailed" or "caped" tortoise (*minogame*), looking up from the left corner of the garment, and two sets of bamboo leaves set in the large open space at the right. A motif of a large crane and tortoise was popular on yogi and is also seen in the occasional silk yogi made in *yūzen* technique (a pattern book published in 1688, *Yūzen hiinagata*, includes a yogi motif of a gigantic flying crane and tortoise). Typically, broad white lines outline the large figures and set them off against a solid blue ground to produce a powerful, unambiguous design. The pigments of the crane, certainly once bright, have faded through long use into lovely pale hues adding to the charm of the piece. The upper leg of the crane extends over the shoulder, bringing the pattern to the front of the garment. Whether this is deliberate or not, it creates a rather sophisticated sense of continuity in the crane design.

4. *Yogi*   (p. 66)

Kyushu Island, early 20th century

Cotton, hand woven, plain weave, rice-paste resist, painted with pigments, dip-dyed in indigo

Natural white, light indigo blue, orange, grey, brown and yellow-brown on dark indigo blue

Kimono construction with gussets; 12½" panel

l. (hem to neck) 59" (150 cm.); collar 2½" (6 cm.); w. (sleeve to sleeve) 48" (122 cm.)

Honolulu Academy of Arts, purchase, 1984 (#5247.1)

This bridal bedding cover, from a late period, has the triangular gussets characteristic of yogi, but it is smaller than usual. It does not have the customary narrow panel inserted at the back. A colorful phoenix painted with pigments, one of the most popular wedding motifs, alights amidst paulownia leaves. Long tail feathers cascade like flowers or ribbons and mingle with scroll-like vine patterns (*karakusa*, Chinese grasses). The swirling rhythm of the grass adds to this yogi an extra decorative touch. In Chinese legend, the phoenix is a hybrid of goose, unicorn, snake, fish (or dragon), tortoise, swallow, and chicken. The circling, undulating, and dotted white tsutsugaki lines render a rather naive quality to this mythic bird. A large family crest in light blue and white at the top balances the spreading bird design at the bottom. On the inner crest three narrow swordlike shapes (*tsurugi*) alternate with three heart-shaped wood-sorrel leaves (*katabami*), hence the crest's name *tsurugi katabami*. The fertility and fast-growing properties of wood sorrel, along with the martial sword, made this an especially prized crest among samurai. Long after the samurai class was abolished, the tsurugi katabami crest (perhaps belonging to the bride's family) became a focal point for this commoner's bridal yogi.

5. *Yogi* (p. 67)

Western Japan, Meiji period (1868–1912)

Cotton, hand woven, plain weave, rice-paste resist, painted with pigments, dip-dyed in indigo and natural yellow dye

Natural white, rose, grey, yellow, orange, moss green, and light blue on green ground

Kimono construction with extra central panel and gussets; 13½″ panel

l. (hem to neck) 62″ (157 cm.); collar 2½″ (6 cm.); w. (sleeve to sleeve) 60″ (152 cm.)

Collection of John and Barbara Stephan

This spectacular piece has a deep green background, probably created by dip-dyeing first in indigo and then in yellow (possibly phellodendron, *kihada,* or miscanthus, *kariyasu.*). After indigo blue, green and brown were the favorite colors for ceremonial tsutsugaki textiles. Auspicious objects from the Noh play *Okina* are gathered together in this yogi design, suggesting a festive occasion—the New Year or a wedding: Noh flute and rounded drum body (right) and drum heads (left), typical pointed hat (*kensaki eboshi*) of the comic dancer Sanbasō (upper right), as well as an opened fan and cluster of hand bells (center left and right) carried by characters in this most auspicious of all Noh plays. The lacquer box at the center, *menbako* (mask box), would be known by viewers to contain the beautiful white mask for the old man, Okina, and the black mask worn by the actor playing Sanbasō. The simple composition contains several symbols of happiness and longevity. Pine branches frame the box on which cherry blossoms bloom. A crane crest decorates the fan and chrysanthemums are painted on the body of the drum. The huge ideographic family crest upper center (*kashiwa,* oak) may indicate one character of a family name or business. The contrast between the bold white areas of the crest against the deep moss-green ground is striking.

6. *Futonji* (p. 68)

Kyushu Island, mid-19th century

Cotton, hand spun, hand woven, plain weave, rice-paste resist, painted pigments, dip-dyed in indigo

Natural white, red, blue, grey on indigo blue

Four-panel construction; 14″ panel

l. 65″ (165 cm.); w. 52″ (132 cm.)

Honolulu Academy of Arts, purchase, 1984 (#5245.1)

This once elegant piece has been used and washed many times, until most of the pigments have lost their brightness. The indigo-blue ground has faded to a light blue. Yet the restful design of the auspicious inhabitants of Mount Hōrai, the everlasting land, is as clear as ever. The piece depicts the standard elements of Mount Hōrai in a typical manner. Two straight bamboo grow at the center, a thick, curving pine tree inhabits the bottom, a crane flies above, and a tortoise supports the earth below. Conventionally shaped five-fingered pine-needle clusters, bamboo leaves, and plum blossoms fill in the rest of the legendary world. The crane and the tortoise are carefully rendered with fine *tsutsu* lines. The tortoise has the gentle head of an animal, not the fierce dragon head as depicted in the following plate. Mount Hōrai is one of the most colorful and decorative motifs, and for that reason it was always popular on wedding bed covers. The serene quality and careful craftsmanship typical of early tsutsugaki works is evident in this piece.

7. *Futonji*   (p. 59)
Kyushu Island, Meiji period (1868–1912)
Cotton, hand spun, hand woven, plain weave, rice-paste resist, painted
   pigments, dip-dyed in indigo
Natural white, red, lavender, grey, khaki on dark indigo blue
Four-panel construction; $12\frac{1}{2}''$ panel
l. 69″ (175 cm.); w. $50\frac{1}{2}''$ (128 cm.)
Honolulu Academy of Arts, purchase, 1985 (#5344.1)

This bright and lively piece probably has not been used since it covered its first owners on their wedding night. In mint condition, it shows the original brilliance of its happy, felicitous motif. The composite design contains the five auspicious inhabitants of Mount Hōrai in Chinese legend—pine, bamboo, plum, and crane and tortoise (*tsuru kame*)—here spreading in a purely Japanese fashion across the deep blue ground. Two bamboo, symbol of resilience, grow straight through the center. The pine tree, symbol of longevity, grows in an undulating curve between the two bamboo and then disappears unexpectedly only to reappear again behind an auspicious crane. (The tsutsugaki craftsman may have forgotten to continue the pine trunk or simply chose to ignore logic.) The plum, symbol of bravery, extends its branches from an unseen trunk in all directions while rows of pink blossoms spread the fragrance of wisdom. The crane descends with open wings from the top and the long-tailed tortoise supports the joyful world of the newlyweds from below. The tortoise is depicted with a dragon head, an additional auspicious element. The red, lavender, khaki, and grey are distributed over the surface of the piece in a purely decorative manner and for the sake of design. The effect is a dazzling, rhythmic display of color against a dark blue ground.

8. *Futonji*   (p. 69)
Saga Prefecture, Kyushu Island, Meiji period (1868–1912)
Cotton, hand spun, hand woven, plain weave, rice-paste resist, painted
   pigments, dip-dyed in indigo, ink calligraphy
Natural white, red, grey, brown, and light blue on dark indigo blue

Four-panel construction; $12\frac{1}{2}''$ panel
l. 69″ (175 cm.); w. 50″ (127 cm.)
Honolulu Academy of Arts, purchase, 1985 (#5336.1)

A late example of the Mount Hōrai motif, in which numerous large figures and extremely elaborated design elements compete for our attention. The serene stability of the earlier Mount Hōrai example (Plate 6) is replaced here with a festive busyness. This gathering of active cranes and tortoises seems to make even the everlasting world appear crowded. Hōrai's peak is dwarfed by its surroundings and scarcely rises above typical ocean waves that recall *ukiyo-e* prints. Two long-tailed tortoises appear to walk on the waves, swaying long sea-grass tails that are decoratively divided into three. The tortoise on the right extends its head of unusual shape that has little in common with the innocent tortoise head of Plate 6 or the dragon head of Plate 7. In the mouth of the companion tortoise on the left is an open Japanese dancing fan inscribed with four ideographs that read "Happiness as High as the Southern Mountain." Three cranes fly joyfully overhead. The center crane carries in its beak an open fan inscribed "Happiness as Deep as the Eastern Ocean." Branches from a slanting pine trunk extend like a canopy over the scene below. Needle clusters are shown as conventionalized, decorative circles that look more like flower blossoms than the pine needles in other designs. Bamboo leaves and plum blossoms, two other elements of the Hōrai motif, appear as insignificant filler between the two worlds of tortoise and crane. There is an even distribution of red, grey, and brown pigments over the whole design suggesting a decorative inclination of the craftsman.

9. *Futonji*   (p. 60)
Okayama Prefecture, early 19th century
Cotton, hand spun, hand woven, plain weave, rice-paste resist, painted
     pigments, dip-dyed in indigo
Natural white, red, pale orange, grey, black, and blue on dark indigo blue
Four-panel construction; 13″ panel
l. 68½″ (174 cm.); w. 54″ (137 cm.)
Honolulu Academy of Arts, purchase, 1937 (#4297)

In this typical *karajishi botan* design a Chinese lion is skillfully caught posed in midstride between enormous peony blossoms. The animal's energy flows outward in stylized, swirling, flamelike designs of hair from the head, legs, and tail of this magical beast. The craftsman who created this festive wedding bed cover probably drew the same design many times; the tsutsu strokes are assured and bring a clear expression to the small face of the lion, in spite of an otherwise conventional rendering. The oversized red and white peony blossoms, symbol of femininity, enclose the lion in lush embrace, while he, the male, is shown in cool colors of grey, black, blue, and white. The red tongue adds a hint of fierceness to this male symbol. The light blue shades of peony leaves and pinwheel designs on the coat of the lion have been created by brushing on indigo pigment rather than by dip-dyeing.

10. *Futonji* (p. 61)
Kyushu Island, 1868–88
Cotton, hand spun, hand woven, plain weave, rice-paste resist, painted
    pigments, dip-dyed in indigo
Natural white, red, grey, brown, yellow, purple, and light blue on indigo
    blue
Five-panel construction; $13\frac{1}{2}''$ panel
l. $74\frac{1}{2}''$ (189 cm.); w. $62\frac{1}{2}''$ (158 cm.)
Honolulu Academy of Arts, purchase, 1984 (#5244.1)

This spectacular piece is unusually large and was probably made to cover
both bride and bridegroom. The Chinese lion and peonies motif, derived
from the Noh drama *Stone Bridge* (*Shakkyō*), fills the entire surface of the
fabric. A ferocious lion with swirling hair is caught in midleap as he plays
among masses of colorful peony flowers set within a mountain scene.
Splashing waterfalls of indigo blue, craggy rocks outlined with broad
white tsutsu lines, and the colored blossoms burst with an energy that
seems to be holding and supporting the central figure of the virile lion.
The profusion of colorful designs crowd against the edges of the fabric,
leaving none of the restful open spaces that are usual in tsutsugaki textiles
(compare with the preceding plate where a smaller lion and peonies
appear against an open blue ground). The craftsmanship of the piece is
extraordinary. Produced in Kyushu, the style has overtones of Kaga
yūzen.

11. *Futonji* (p. 62)
Kyushu Island, late 18th or early 19th century
Cotton, hand spun, hand woven, plain weave, rice-paste resist, painted
    pigments, dip-dyed in indigo
Natural white, pale red, light orange, and grey on indigo blue
Four-panel construction; $13''$ panel
l. $58''$ (147 cm.); w. $51''$ (129 cm.)
Honolulu Academy of Arts, purchase, 1937 (#4338)

A delicate-colored phoenix spreads its tail majestically as it seems to settle
onto its perch in a paulownia tree. The mythical bird is decorated with
exceptionally fine tsutsu lines, forming elaborate and detailed patterns
reminiscent of embroidery stitches. Varied pigments of red, orange, and
grey have been brushed over the body, wings, head, and tail feathers.
Once probably brilliant, these colors are now faded into pleasantly mellow
shades. The paulownia leaves are equally decorative, being made in
varied patterns. The insect holes in the leaves, often seen in Kaga yūzen
pieces, add a realistic touch to the mythical scene. The gentle shading
effects in the blossoms, leaves, and tail feathers indicate the unusual
sophistication of this early tsutsugaki textile.

12. *Futonji,* altered from *yogi* (p. 70)
Saga Prefecture, Kyushu Island, mid-19th century
Cotton, hand spun, hand woven, plain weave, rice-paste resist, painted
    with pigments, dip-dyed in indigo
Light blue, red, orange, orange-brown, and grey on deep indigo blue
Four-and-a-half-panel construction; 12½″ panel
l. 93½″ (238 cm.); w. 57″ (145 cm.)
Honolulu Academy of Arts, purchase, 1937 (#4303)

It is likely that this colorful piece, now a flat hanging, was once the back
and a part of the front of a yogi. The alteration of a used or damaged
yogi into a smaller textile was common. That the piece was originally
a yogi is suggested by the narrow center panel, characteristic of yogi,
and more especially by the pieced-in section of the center panel above
the head of the phoenix, which marks the neck opening in the original
kimono shape. The feathers that now spread upward in the air originally
cascaded down the front panels of the yogi and would not have been seen
together with the rest of the pattern. The auspicious phoenix is bril-
liantly colored and its spread feathers intermingle with conventional
karakusa patterns (see Plate 4). The bird is seen in its legendary nesting
place, indicated by a single bunch of paulownia leaves at the bottom of
the motif. Three spikes of paulownia flowers undulate in curves that
repeat, in small scale, the space-filling arcs of the phoenix's feathers above
them. The brilliant coloring of this piece may have been influenced by
the *bingata* dyeing of Okinawa.

13. *Futonji* (p. 71)
Saga Prefecture, Kyushu Island, Meiji period (1868–1912)
Cotton, hand spun, hand woven, plain weave, rice-paste resist, painted
    pigments, dip-dyed in indigo
Natural white, orange, red, blue-green, grey, sky blue, and brown on
    dark indigo blue
Four-panel construction; 14″ panel
l. 63″ (160 cm.); w. 52″ (132 cm.)
Honolulu Academy of Arts, purchase, 1937 (#4298)

This bright, joyful depiction of a majestic phoenix with open wings,
perched in a paulownia tree, presents a concentrated, powerful image.
The tsutsu lines are wide and the colors strong, opaque and boldly con-
trastive. The paulownia tree is large and undulating, swirling with energy. Its leaves and flowers are formed into patterns as conventionalized
as crests. The wonderful delicacy of the phoenix-paulownia motif in
earlier tsutsugaki (Plate 11, for example) is not evident. The craftsman
has followed largely conventional forms (the curls of the neck feathers,
for example) in rendering the phoenix, yet the overall effect is of a living
bird caught in motion. The upright feather in the center of the composition, instead of streaming down with the others, suddenly stops at
the edge of the cover, disturbing the balance of the composition (com-

pare with the careful design of the earlier piece). One understated element of the design is the small spray of bamboo leaves, another companion of the phoenix, inconspicuously growing at the base of the paulownia tree.

14. *Futonji,* altered from *yogi* (p. 72)
Okayama Prefecture, late 18th or early 19th century
Cotton, hand spun, hand woven, plain weave, rice-paste resist, painted with pigments, dip-dyed in indigo
Pale orange, grey, and light blue on indigo blue
Four-and-a-half-panel construction; 12½″ panel
l. 51½″ (131 cm.); w. 46″ (117 cm.)
Honolulu Academy of Arts, purchase, 1937 (#4336)

This delicate and restrained early textile was once the back of a yogi—note the central panel and small horizontal seam above the crest indicating the neck line. It boasted this huge family crest of *mukaichō,* a pattern of two facing butterflies whose wings gently and lovingly touch—an appropriate image for a sleeping cover for newlyweds. Butterfly crests were a favorite of the samurai class, their beauty and fragility representing elegance and courtly grace which the warrior longed for in his harsh life. Butterfly crests became popular as well among commoners, especially Kabuki actors and courtesans. Here, against a blue background, a single crest of fragile butterflies becomes an entire motif and presents a strong image: soft shades of persimmon and grey within finely drawn symmetrical wings contrast with the boldness of the single motif. The crest design here may have been a family emblem; or it may have been used by the tsutsugaki craftsman as a purely decorative element deemed appropriate to the new tie of bride and groom.

15. *Futonji,* probably altered from *yogi* (p. 73)
Shikoku Island, Meiji period (1868–1912)
Cotton, hand spun, hand woven, plain weave, rice-paste resist, stencil- and cone-drawn patterns, painted with pigments, dip-dyed in indigo, natural yellow dye
Natural white, light blue on blue-green
Four-and-a-half-panel construction; 13″ panel
l. 61½″ (155 cm.); w. 54″ (137 cm.)
Honolulu Academy of Arts, purchase, 1985 (#5341.1)

Cycad palms (*sotetsu*) grow wild in warm regions of Japan—Kyushu, Okinawa, Shikoku. These tropical plants are also raised as ornamental plants. The sotetsu design occasionally appears in kimono and other decorative arts. In this textile from Shikoku four cycad palms are naturalistically rendered. Some fronds are drawn with unusual, broad, tapered strokes of the tsutsu resembling calligraphic brush strokes. In contrast, the scales of the bark and some fronds have been drawn with extremely fine tsutsu lines. Light blue on the trunks and some fronds suggests shadows while the natural white seems to represent highlights. Above the sotetsu plants is an enormous mokkō family crest encircled by four decorative petals. The entire white inner surface of the crest is covered with a pattern of dots within circles (*kanoko*). Kanoko were originally made by binding and dyeing, but when the expensive tie-dye technique was prohibited by government edict, a stencil came to be used to create the same effect, as seen here. A stencil cut in the dot-circle pattern was placed on the cloth and rice paste was applied through the openings in the stencil. An initial dyeing in indigo produced light blue dots, after which the entire crest was covered with rice paste prior to final dyeing. Yellow natural dyes were then applied to make the unusual blue-green ground. The kanoko crest was in vogue in the nineteenth century, when many decorative variations of family crests were invented for rich merchants, courtesans, and Kabuki actors. This unique country bedding cover boasts an impressive and embellished crest that suits the festive wedding occasion.

16. *Futonji,* probably altered from *yogi* (p. 74)
Western Japan, Meiji period (1868–1912)
Cotton, hand spun, hand woven, plain weave, rice-paste resist, painted
  with pigments, dip-dyed in indigo
Natural white, pale shades of grey, orange, brown, and light blue on
  indigo blue
Four-and-a-half-panel construction; 13½″ panel
l. 57″ (145 cm.); w. 58″ (147 cm.)
Private Collection, Honolulu

Under a stark *hanabishi* (flower in diamond) family crest, an auspicious plum tree bearing clumps of pale blossoms reaches out to both sides from a solid base shaded by bamboo leaves that float on delicate, curving bamboo stalks. The pine—the third traditional auspicious plant in shō-chikubai designs—is not included here. The precision of the composition and exact technical execution of the design suggests there was a painterly prototype. Assertive white tsutsu lines, without any mark of hesitation, outline the tree, flowers, and leaves. Although the motif is decorative, it also possesses a natural feeling. The sensitive shading from pink to white and from grey to white of the blossoms suggests natural coloring. The trunk of the plum tree, on the other hand, is dyed in flat light indigo blue. The peculiar juxtaposition of naturalistic shading and conventional flat-color design in one motif does not spoil the loveliness of this country tsutsugaki bed cover; on the contrary, the contrast is pleasantly stimulating to the imagination. The simple clarity of the design is a delight.

17. *Futonji,* probably altered from *yogi* (p. 63)
Probably Shikoku Island, Meiji period (1868–1912)
Cotton, hand spun, hand woven, plain weave, rice-paste resist, dip-dyed
  in indigo

Natural white and light blue on deep indigo blue
Four-and-a-half-panel construction; $14\frac{1}{2}''$ panel
l. 63" (160 cm.); w. $61\frac{1}{2}''$ (154 cm.)
Honolulu Academy of Arts, purchase, 1985 (#5340.1)

Four auspicious minogame, symbols of longevity, are skillfully rendered with tsutsu lines. The sophisticated placement of the four animals within the design and the utter assurance of the handling of the tsutsu in the depiction of the heads of the two large tortoises offer abundant evidence that the maker of this piece was a consummate artist within the dye medium. Each of the four animals is rendered differently. In using merely white and two shades of blue the craftsman shows how much variety can be achieved with imagination and skill of workmanship. The dark indigo blue of the ground is cleverly incorporated into the shell patterns of the two large tortoises, patterns which are color opposites of each other (a pair, male and female, may be suggested). The two small tortoises (the head of one is lost through damage to the textile) soften the design and add a playful touch. Each tortoise tail is drawn differently—broad white; flowing; thin; bunched. A craftsman produces precise effects like this using a single dye source by carefully planning each step of the design-dye process in advance. The wood-sorrel crest is also meticulously drawn over the auspicious gathering. Sword-blade shapes in the ground color are part of the crest design (see Plate 4).

18. *Futonji,* probably altered from *yogi*   (p. 75).
Western Japan, San'in area, mid- or late-19th century
Cotton, hand spun, hand woven, plain weave, rice-paste resist, dip-dyed
  in indigo
Natural white and light blue on dark indigo blue
Four-and-a-half-panel construction; 13" panel
l. 54" (137 cm.); w. 54" (137 cm.)
Private Collection, Honolulu

Sometimes family crests were grouped into a decorative pattern, as with this three-crest motif on a wedding bed cover. At the top center is an *omodaka* (water plantain) crest, perhaps of the bride's family, which was once popular among samurai families. The water-plantain leaf has an unusual three-pointed shape. The tall-stemmed plant grows in marshes and blooms with spikes of small, three-petaled flowers in the summer time. The plant's unique shape and its popular name "victory grass" (*shōgunsō*) appealed to warriors of an earlier time, and later to commoners as well. Beneath this crest a pair of open-winged cranes join to celebrate the marriage occasion. The auspicious crane is a symbol of longevity, companion to the long-lived tortoise on many designs. The cranes form circular crests that are nearly identical. The birds face each other fiercely alert but the slight difference in their expressions—one has his beak resolutely closed, the other aggressively open—creates an amusing little drama. We can only guess whether the country craftsman was making an intentional comment on the marriage occasion or was simply drawing two expressive birds. Working with a palette of only white and two shades of indigo blue, the artist has, in any event, fashioned a starkly beautiful image on this rather unusual bedding cover.

19. *Futonji* (p. 64)
Ehime or Kagawa Prefecture, Shikoku Island, early 19th century
Cotton, hand spun, hand woven, plain weave, rice-paste resist, painted
  pigments, dip-dyed in indigo
Natural white, pale grey, and pale ochre on indigo blue
Four-panel construction; 13½″ panel
l. 61″ (155 cm.); w. 51″ (129 cm.)
Honolulu Academy of Arts, purchase, 1952 (#1545.1)

The tea ceremony developed as a subculture of Zen Buddhism among samurai in the sixteenth century and later among townsmen. In the simple art of *wabicha,* originated by Sen Rikyū, a few carefully selected and often expensive tea articles were all that met the eye in the humble and isolated room in which the tea ceremony was practiced. In time tea classes became fashionable training for young girls, and tea objects became an occasional decoration, especially on Shikoku Island, for tsutsugaki bridal bed covers. On this lovely early piece, tea utensils and related objects are arranged around a dominating ivy (*tsuta*) crest, perhaps the most popular of all family crests. The objects face the center, hence some appear upside down. Looking counterclockwise from the top of the left panel: a hanging picture scroll, probably of an innocent-faced, humorous Daruma (Bodhidharma), the first Zen patriarch; a teaspoon and a trivet for a kettle; a miniature mountain landscape on a round tray (not directly related to the tea ceremony), charcoal in a pan, and small ash rake; probably a charcoal holder and charcoal tongs, trivet, and iron ring-handles of a tea kettle; a tea whisk, dustpan, and plum flower; a square, legged tobacco tray holding a bamboo ashtray in which two feathers for brushing ashes are standing and two pieces of burning charcoal for lighting pipes, and beside it a trivet; two pieces of charcoal; sticks of charcoal in a basket with a handle; two tea containers and two long-handled teaspoons; and a kettlelike object and flower. Tea-ceremony utensils often were depicted in tsutsugaki textiles as if transparent, showing the inside of the object. Perhaps the two charcoal pieces inside the tobacco tray (lower right) appear through this convention.

20. *Futonji* (p. 76)
Collected in Akita Prefecture, late 18th or early 19th century
Cotton, hand spun, hand woven, plain weave, rice-paste resist, dip-dyed
  in indigo
Natural white, light indigo blue on dark indigo blue
Five-panel construction; 12″ panel

l. 59″ (150 cm.); w. 54″ (137 cm.)
Honolulu Academy of Arts, purchase, 1937 (#4337)

Not many tsutsugaki textiles made in Japan's northeast region have survived. This serene blue and white bed cover has been attributed to Akita
Prefecture in northern Japan. However, the simple light blue and white
colors and the design of scattered crests are more common in tsutsugaki
cottons made in the Izumo area of Shimane Prefecture. Nine crests of
different sizes are arranged in slightly uneven rows setting up a delightful
rhythm of asymmetry. Auspicious plants, trees, flowers, and animals are
gathered into a family of medallion-like crests, each celebrating married
life. Starting with the top row from the left are: chrysanthemum blossoms; crane; pine (all longevity); paulownia (the phoenix's companion);
plum (bravery and wisdom); bamboo (resilience); peony flowers (femininity); tortoise (longevity and stability); and iris (beauty and fragrance).
These highly ornamental crests were probably selected for their design
and symbolic value and were unrelated to family crests of the bride or
groom.

21. *Futonji*   (p. 77)
Kumamoto Prefecture, last half of the 19th century
Cotton, hand spun, hand woven, plain weave, rice-paste resist, painted
    pigments, dip-dyed in indigo
Natural white, light blue, orange, grey-brown on indigo blue
Four-panel construction; 13″ panel
l. 64½″ (162 cm.); w. 51″ (130 cm.)
Honolulu Academy of Arts, purchase, 1985 (#5334.1)

The *tatewaku* (vertical frame) design of undulating vertical lines that
enclose motifs, first developed as a weaving pattern used for high-ranking
courtiers' costumes (*yūsokumon*). A woven tatewaku pattern usually had
one repeated motif such as clouds, bamboo, waves, or wisteria. In this
ceremonial bed cover, the old and aristocratic woven pattern is adapted
to the dyeing process: a medley of five traditional festive motifs in
miniature size are arranged within four pairs of undulating vertical lines
in varied order. The motifs are: a peony blossom with karakusa vines; a
crane and a pine branch; a tortoise and waves; bamboo leaves; and chrysanthemum flowers. Two double *takanoha* (falcon feather) family crests in
the top corners of the piece probably were balanced by two similar crests
in the bottom corners now missing. The falcon feather resembled the
feathers of an arrow and suggested a warrior's love of falconry. It was a
favorite samurai crest as well as a crest associated with Shinto shrines.
Although the pigments have been rubbed away now, the sensitive
manner in which the artisan wielded an extremely fine tsutsu is notable.
Details of the crane feathers, tortoise shell, and peony petals are meticulously crafted. Tiny white dots, made with an extra-fine tsutsu embellish
the motifs, adding an especially delicate effect of splashing waves and
snow falling on bamboo.

22. *Futonji*   (p. 78)
Probably Shimane Prefecture, early 19th century
Cotton, hand spun, hand woven, plain weave, rice-paste resist, dip-dyed
    in indigo
Natural white and light indigo blue on dark indigo blue
Four-panel construction; 13½″ panel
l. 57″ (145 cm.); w. 50″ (127 cm.)
Honolulu Academy of Arts, purchase, 1952 (#1546.1)

Good-luck symbols have always been favorite subjects for textile design
in Japan and China. Ten precious objects decorate this bed cover to
celebrate the happy start of a new married life. They are associated with
the Treasure Ship (*takarabune*) and its passengers, the Seven Lucky Gods
(*shichi fukujin*). The design in decorative art is known as the Collection
of Treasures (*takara zukushi*). From the left and from top to bottom, they
are: hiding cape (*kakuremino*) in the shape of leaves that makes its wearer
invisible; flaming treasure pearl (*hōju*), which makes wishes come true;
orange flower and leaves (*tachibana*) promising succulent fruit; mallet of
good fortune (*uchide no kozuchi*) whose blow produces wealth; Seven
Treasures (*shippō*) in lozenge shape; treasure key (*takarakagi*) to unlock
the treasure house; cloves (*chōji*) in elongated, pointed form whose fra-
grant blossoms are burned to purify the air; hiding hat (*kakuregasa*), which,
like the cape, makes its wearer invisible; merchant's weights (*fundō*) made
of gold or silver; and a money bag (*kanebukuro*), which keeps and produces wealth. The small, irregularly placed designs cheerfully stand out
from, rather than fill, the dark background.

23. *Futonji*   (p. 79)
Probably Shikoku Island, Meiji period (1868–1912)
Cotton, hand spun, hand woven, plain weave, rice-paste resist, dip-dyed
    in indigo, painted natural yellow dye
Natural white, light indigo blue on green
Three-panel construction; 13″ panel
l. 59″ (150 cm.); w. 36″ (91 cm.)
Honolulu Academy of Arts, purchase, 1985 (#5338.1)

A bed cover made of three kimono-widths of material was usually used
as a bottom spread (*shikibuton*). This unusual piece may originally have
been a full four-width bed cover. The usual bottom spread was dyed
solid blue and rarely boasted crests or other pictorial motifs. This delightful piece is decorated with homey objects of Japanese domestic life.
On the left panel are a three-pronged horse radish, humorously suggesting fertility, and an ordinary grater, its handle embellished by tassels that
add an auspicious and decorative flavor to the simple design. On the
middle panel are a smoking pipe, deep ashtray, and tobacco pouch with
a cord to be tucked into the sash. The right panel shows a collection of
tea-ceremony utensils: a round object that may be a small cup; a ladle;
whisk for stirring; tea grinder and plum branch; and a teaspoon. The

obvious naïveté and humor with which the artisan drew the designs with a tsutsu make this a unique bed cover. It is a charming work from the hands of a country tsutsugaki craftsman. Unusual red basting stitches sewn down the two center seams make a contrast against the green ground.

24. *Futonji* (p. 80)
Western Japan, Meiji period (1868–1912)
Cotton, hand spun, hand woven, plain weave, rice-paste resist, direct ink
  painting, painted pigments, dip-dyed in indigo
Natural white, light blue, grey, and rose on indigo blue
Four-panel construction; 12½″ panel
l. 57″ (145 cm.); w. 47″ (119 cm.)
Collection of Alex and Sandy Anderson, Honolulu

The folding fan is a cherished invention of the Japanese. Since Heian times a large folding fan made of linked cypress slats has been an essential part of the attire of a court noble. Fans made of polished bamboo ribs covered with paper are much admired for their beauty and have many practical uses. Often they are painted with motifs or auspicious symbols. An opened fan (*suehiro*) is a frequent decorative pattern in Japanese art; symbolizing an opening future, it is highly auspicious. In this bed cover, three spread-fan shapes are casually drawn by freehand tsutsu, their slight irregularity contributing to the country feeling of the piece. Auspicious scenes on the fans combine two contrasting styles. On the right fan a small crane, spreading its feathers among pine clusters and small waves, is drawn with ink in minute detail. The left fan carries two images: a bold closeup of a pine tree's midsection that has been spontaneously drawn with a tsutsu and, sheltered beneath large needle clusters, three tiny houses and distant mountains touched with brown pigment. The latter scene is delicately inked, in the same style as the crane. A similar juxtaposition of boldness and detail is seen in the center fan as well: rough, gnarled plum trees contrast with rocks and yellow-grey blossoms that are ink-drawn in painterly detail. Below the fans, two well-known motifs in the form of large decorative crests anchor the design—auspicious bamboo on the right and tortoise and wave on the left. Light indigo blue from the fabric's initial dyeing is used effectively to create the bamboo, pine needles, tortoise, and wave within the design. The dark blue of the final indigo dyeing has been skillfully integrated into the bamboo crest and fan designs.

25. *Futonji* (p. 89)
Kyushu Island, mid-19th century
Cotton, hand woven, plain weave, rice-paste resist, painted pigments,
  dip-dyed in indigo
Natural white, red, green, light blue, grey, yellow, and brown on dark
  indigo blue

Four-panel construction; 13″ panel
l. 64″ (162 cm.); w. 51″ (129 cm.)
Honolulu Academy of Arts, purchase, 1937 (#4339)

Against a stark blue-black ground, five colorful cranes in varied realistic postures gather to celebrate an auspicious occasion. The well-balanced composition and lively rendering suggests the artisan may have been following a painter's cartoon. The strong combination of opaque colors —red, yellow, green—in the bodies of the cranes is somewhat disturbing. Nevertheless, a wedding bed cover with a design of five auspicious cranes, symbolizing abundant happiness and longevity, was certain to have been prized. The extremely dark blackish blue ground was probably made by painting the cloth with lampblack mixed into liquid soybean before dip-dyeing in indigo.

26. *Futonji* (p. 90)
Yamagata Prefecture, Meiji period (1868–1912)
Cotton, hand spun, hand woven, plain weave, rice-paste resist, dip-dyed
   in indigo
Natural white and light blue on dark indigo blue
Four-panel construction; 14″ panel
l. 61½″ (154 cm.); w. 52½″ (133 cm.)
Honolulu Academy of Arts, purchase, 1985 (#5335.1)

Oversized *noshi* (ceremonial dried abalone) and *hōju* (treasure pearl) motifs are dramatically combined in the design of this wedding bed cover. Noshi is dried abalone stretched into long ribbonlike strips. Because the sound of the word also means "prolong," it became customary to include noshi with a gift as a symbol of longevity and prolonged happiness. (The custom continues today, strips of yellow paper or printed images usually substituting for the abalone itself.) The *abarenoshi* (wild-abalone strips) motif, seen here, suggesting good fortune in many directions, was a popular auspicious pattern in decorative arts. Hōju, associated with esoteric Buddhism, is usually shown within a flame or cloudlike pattern. It is also called "wish-come-true pearl" (*nyoihōju*), for it is reputed to fulfill any wish. The large center pearl here is flanked by a smaller pearl on either side and framed by a floating, undulating cloud pattern in light blue. The simple coloring of white and two tones of indigo blue create a dramatic and powerful design.

27. *Futonji* (p. 91)
Possibly Kumamoto (collected in Yonago, Shimane Prefecture), Meiji
   period (1868–1912)
Cotton, hand spun, hand woven, plain weave, rice-paste resist, dip-dyed
   in indigo, ink drawing
Natural white, light blue on deep indigo blue
Four-panel construction; 13″ panel

l. 74″ (198 cm.); w. 49″ (125 cm.)
Honolulu Academy of Arts, purchase, 1984 (#5246.1)

The vinelike karakusa pattern, brought from China and Korea, has been popular in Japan since the Nara period. Two sources for the design have been proposed: lotus and palmetto shapes of ancient Egypt, via Greece and Central Asia, and Chinese twisting dragons that have lost heads and legs. In the course of time peony, grape, paulownia, pine, chrysanthemum, and morning glory were incorporated into fanciful karakusa designs. During the Edo period, simple karakusa designs of a stylized, twisting vine became popular and were used as motifs for ordinary cotton *furoshiki* as well as for ceremonial cloth covers (*yutan*). This unusual piece has a single large white peony flower—a symbol of prosperity—at the center, its petals defined with ink lines. Single karakusa vines radiate out from the peony, making precise energetic curls. The vine is hardy and grows endlessly. So it is a symbol both of progeny and of longevity, and is appropriate for festive occasions. The restless activity of the center is balanced by four family crests of simple mokkō design that anchor the corners. A design with crests in four corners is often seen on tsutsugaki pieces produced in Kumamoto Prefecture.

28. *Yutan* or *Furoshiki* (p. 92)
Probably Okayama Prefecture, early 19th century
Cotton, hand spun, hand woven, plain weave, rice-paste resist, cone
    drawing, stencil, dip-dyed in indigo, brushed ink, direct-ink painting
Natural white and grey on indigo blue and black patterned ground
Four-panel construction; 13″ panel
l. 65″ (165 cm.); w. 50″ (127 cm.)
Honolulu Academy of Arts, gift of Mrs. Theodore A. Cooke, 1937
    (#4305)

An overall repeated pattern created by stencil was commonly applied to everyday bed covers. This unusual piece, probably a chest cover or wrapping cloth, combines an everyday stencil pattern with a large auspicious crane crest in the center. The outline of the crane was drawn with a tsutsu and the entire crane design covered with rice paste before immersing the fabric briefly in indigo to get a ground color of light blue. After the fabric was dry another coat of rice was applied through a floral-pattern stencil. Dark black ink was brushed over the entire fabric surface that remained exposed. When the rice paste was washed off, the crane's feathers and highly expressive face were painted in ink directly onto the cloth. (Or the ink painting could have been done before dip-dyeing.) The result is a striking configuration of black, white, and light-blue designs, in which the eye of the crane in the center is the focal point.

29. *Yutan* or *Noren* (p. 93)
North-central Japan (Kanazawa area or north of Kyoto), second quarter of 19th century
Cotton, hand spun, hand woven, plain weave, rice-paste resist, dip-dyed in indigo
Natural white and light blue on indigo blue
Three-panel construction; 13½″
l. 60½″ (154 cm.); w. 38″ (97 cm.)
Honolulu Academy of Arts, purchase, 1937 (#4299)

An orthodox pine, bamboo, plum motif is elegantly drawn and colored in simple blue and white. Beautifully shaped plum blossoms and buds and pine-needle clusters form a middle and an upper tier of the design, while bamboo leaves surround the base of strongly delineated pine and plum trunks. This is an auspicious textile obviously created for some festive occasion; its use, however, is not clear. It may have been a curtain or used as a bureau or chest cover.

30. *Furoshiki* (p. 94)
Probably Shikoku Island, Meiji period (1868–1912)
Cotton, hand spun, hand woven, plain weave, rice-paste resist, painted pigments, dip-dyed in indigo, brushed natural yellow dye
Natural white, light blue, grey, and orange on light blue-green
Four-panel construction; 13″ panel
l. 62″ (157 cm.); w. 53½″ (136 cm.)
Honolulu Academy of Arts, purchase, 1985 (#5339.1)

The chrysanthemum is known in both China and Japan as one of the "four princes" (*shikunshi*) in the world of art, along with the plum, bamboo, and orchid. The flower is also known as "sunburst" (*nikka*) and "sun spirit" (*nissei*) because its petals radiate outward like the rays of the sun. In Chinese legend chrysanthemum tea ensures longevity. The flower's September festival was especially favored by Kyoto's aristocrats, who drank chrysanthemum wine to celebrate longevity. The designs on this furoshiki reflect the auspicious tradition of the chrysanthemum festival by linking the blossoms with a wine cup. Different types of chrysanthemum bloom in the corners of the design. The especially auspicious ideograph *kotobuki* (happiness) appears in three variations: broad, clear strokes in the lower right; slender, pointed strokes suggestive of a castle or a crane in the upper left (where it appears upside down); and in highly abstract form as a wine cup adjoining the flower in the bottom left. The large family crest at the center of the piece comprises a square diamond-flower design surrounded by four pairs of intertwined wisteria.

31. *Furoshiki* or *Yutan* (p. 81)
Probably Okayama Prefecture, early 19th century
Cotton, hand spun, hand woven, plain weave, rice-paste resist, painted
    pigments, dip-dyed in indigo
Natural white, pale pink, grey, brown, red-brown, and blue on indigo
    blue
Four-panel construction; 14½″ panel
l. 65″ (165 cm.); w. 56″ (142 cm.)
Honolulu Academy of Arts, purchase, 1937 (#4295)

A mythical phoenix appears majestically in the center of this remarkable
ceremonial cloth in the circular form of a family crest. Details of the
feathers are elaborately rendered through fine tsutsu lines and brushed
pigments. An elegant mood is created by subtle shading of colors, from
dark hues to pastels. The design is complemented and lightened by karakusa patterns that swirl around the rather formal figure of the phoenix.
This large, elegant furoshiki was probably used to wrap or to cover a
bride's belongings during the ceremonies of marriage.

32. *Furoshiki* (p. 82)
Kyushu Island, early 20th century
Cotton, hand woven, plain weave, rice-paste resist, painted pigments,
    dip-dyed in indigo
Natural white, rose, yellow, grey, and light blue on indigo blue
Three-panel construction; 11″ panel
l. 30″ (76 cm.); w. 31½″ (80 cm.)
Honolulu Academy of Arts, purchase, 1985 (#5345.1)

33. *Furoshiki* (p. 95)
Kyushu Island, early 20th century
Cotton, probably machine woven, plain weave, rice-paste resist, painted
    pigments, dip-dyed in indigo
Natural white, brown, yellow, and light blue on indigo blue
Single-panel construction; 30″ panel
l. 30″ (76 cm.); w. 30″ (76 cm.)
Collection of Mr. George Ellis

34. *Furoshiki* (p. 96)
Western Japan, early 20th century
Cotton, hand woven, plain weave, rice-paste resist, dip-dyed in indigo
Natural white, light blue on indigo blue
Three-panel construction; 13″ panel
l. 48½″ (123cm.); w. 38″ (96 cm.)
Private collection, Honolulu

The three wrapping cloths bear similar motifs. The first two have shōchikubai designs of pine, bamboo, and plum; the design of the third does
not have the plum. In each a strong, rough-barked pine trunk is depicted

by two broad lines of the tsutsu and large irregular spots. Pine-needle clusters are small, single, rounded forms—not the five-segment clusters seen on other pieces. A circular crest (plum, crossed falcon feathers, and double butterfly) decorates the lower right corner of each. The crests are placed upright on these lovely small furoshiki, not in a diagonal position (see Plate 36). The cloths may have been made as covers for auspicious gifts, not intended to be tied, thus explaining the position of the crests. In spite of the similarity of their motifs, each textile is distinct in its workmanship and conveys its own mood.

35. *Furoshiki*   (p. 83)
Kyushu Island, Meiji period (1868–1912)
Cotton, hand spun, hand woven, plain weave, rice-paste resist, painted pigments, dip-dyed in indigo
Natural white, yellow, orange, grey, brown, rose, purple, and light blue on dark indigo blue
Three-panel construction; $13\frac{1}{2}''$ panel
l. 44″ (112 cm.); w. $38\frac{1}{2}''$ (98 cm.)
Private collection, Honolulu

This lovely furoshiki has a motif that is rarely seen in tsutsugaki textiles: mandarin ducks (*oshidori*) among bamboo and snow. Mated mandarin ducks are inseparable. Male and female swim and fly together. They sleep with their heads on each other's breasts. If one bird dies, its companion will not mate again, so it is believed. Thus, in popular imagination, as well as in art and literature, the oshidori symbolizes steadfast love between husband and wife (a loving human couple is called an "oshidori couple"). In this design a pair of ducks plays by a stream, the female splashing in the water while the male preens and calls from the bank close by. Snow falls through the air and weighs down clumps of bamboo leaves. In Japanese decorative arts of the Momoyama and Edo periods the clean and serene image of bamboo laden with snow was a favorite motif. With the resilience, longevity, and love symbolized by the combined motif, this wedding furoshiki presents a truly auspicious meaning. Delicate coloring and careful shading capture the loveliness of the birds. A circular family crest in the lower right corner, made of three open fans, balances the design. The folding fan, a Japanese invention, is an auspicious symbol. Opened wide, it is an apt illustration of human desire for a flourishing future. The three-fan crest in light indigo blue is especially lovely as a part of this rare tsutsugaki composition.

36. *Furoshiki*   (p. 84)
Central Japan (collected in Takayama), Meiji period (1868–1912)
Cotton, hand spun, hand woven, plain weave, rice-paste resist, dip-dyed in indigo
Natural white and light blue on dark indigo blue
Four-panel construction; $13\frac{1}{2}''$ panel

l. 56″ (142 cm.); w. 51″ (130 cm.)
Collection of James R. and Reiko M. Brandon, Honolulu

A clear, decorative *tabane noshi* (joined abalone) motif, in white and light blue, is stunningly set against a deep indigo ground. Auspicious abalone strips, wrapped and tied at the center, spread out in a familiar pattern that is more formal and regular than the wild abalone motif in Plate 26. There is a pleasant symmetry, even elegance, to this mirror-image design. Decorative markings on the white strips probably indicate an uneven or torn texture of the thinly shaved and stretched strips. A double falcon-feather family crest is placed at the bottom left corner in diagonal position (the top of the crest faces the center of the cloth). When the ends of the cloth are folded over a parcel the crest will be properly seen.

37. *Furoshiki*   (p. 97)
Probably Kyushu Island, Meiji period (1868–1912)
Cotton, hand spun, hand woven, plain weave, rice-paste resist, painted
    pigments, dip-dyed in indigo
Natural white, yellow, orange, pink, biege, brown, and grey on indigo
    hlne
Three-panel construction; 13½″ panel
l. 43″ (109 cm.); w. 40″ (102 cm.)
Collection of John and Barbara Stephan

A set of good-luck treasures, cargo of the Treasure Ship, decorates this feminine and cheerful bridal cloth (see also Plate 22). The careful rendering of the colorful treasures includes elaborate embellishments and details. The invisible cape spreads its magical power, here depicted through a few leaves and straw radiating outward. A large money bag decorated with chrysanthemum flowers and leaves dominates the left bottom corner. Balancing it in the upper right is a lucky mallet of grained wood, poised to produce good fortune. Small auspicious symbols are scattered around the cape: two flaming pearls (top left and center right); two cloves (center right); tangerine with leaves and spherical Seven Treasures (center bottom); and a stylized pattern based on crossed scrolls (center left). A furoshiki is usually wrapped around a gift and the ends tied to secure it; however, sometimes it is used as a protective covering that is laid or spread flat over the gift. Probably this cloth was intended to be laid flat on top of a gift. This is suggested by the exceptionally colorful and elaborate design and by the upright position of the crest of three butterflies (not in the usual diagonal tying position).

38. *Yuage*   (p. 98)
Izumo (Shimane Prefecture), Meiji period (1868–1912)
Cotton, hand spun, hand woven, plain weave, rice-paste resist, dip-dyed
    in indigo, natural madder or safflower dye
Light blue and off-white

Two-panel construction; 14″ panel
l. 35″ (89 cm.); w. 26½″ (67 cm.)
Honolulu Academy of Arts, purchase, 1985 (#5343.1)

The dye colors of Izumo tsutsugaki textiles, as if reflecting the severe climate of the area, are sombre—commonly several shades of indigo blue, sometimes blue-green or dark brown. Tsutsugaki baby towels, however, had a bright red triangle in the upper right corner. This part of the towel was traditionally dyed in madder or safflower, medicinal plants as well as dye sources. The baby's face only was wiped with the red area, for it was believed that the red dye prevented smallpox. This baby towel is a wonderful example of how country artisans created simple yet beautiful objects appropriate to their function. The towel's colors are now faded from long use—the red is completely gone—but the felicitous design, executed by the craftsman in sure, direct, uncomplicated strokes, retains its original innocent appeal. An auspicious flying crane and tortoise gently survey the scene and, together with the small pines and bamboo, offer their protection to the new infant. It is said that the long, closed beak of a crane on an Izumo baby towel was a humorous hint from the grandparents that they wanted a baby boy (an open crane's beak, on the other hand, suggested the female sex).

39. Ceremonial cloth (p. 99)
Western Japan, mid-19th century
Cotton, hand spun, hand woven, plain weave, rice-paste resist, painted pigment, dip-dyed in indigo
Natural white and red on indigo blue
Two-panel construction; 13½″ panel
l. 48″ (122 cm.); w. 26″ (66 cm.)
Honolulu Academy of Arts, purchase, 1937 (#4300)

The purpose of this gentle little textile is not known. It may be a piece from Izumo that celebrated a child's birth (a similar textile in the Yuasa Hachirō Memorial Museum, Tokyo, was made in Izumo). The familiar auspicious couple, the crane and tortoise, fly over and swim in the ocean. The animals are skillfully rendered and in an otherwise simple design their tentative gaze creates minor tension. A touch of rose on the crane's head and in three patterns of the tortoise's shell near the neck give a warm accent to this serene cloth.

40. *Kooi* (p. 100)
Izumo (Shimane Prefecture), Meiji period (1868–1912)
Cotton, hand spun, hand woven, plain weave, rice-paste resist, dip-dyed in indigo
Natural white on indigo blue
Single-panel construction; 12½″ panel

l. 175″ (445 cm.); w. 12½″ (32 cm.)
Honolulu Academy of Arts, purchase, 1985 (#5342.1)

41. *Kooi* (p. 100)
Izumo (Shimane Prefecture), Meiji period (1868–1912)
Cotton, hand spun, hand woven, plain weave, rice-paste resist, dip-dyed
 in indigo
Natural white on indigo blue
Single-panel construction; 12½″ panel
l. 168″ (428 cm.); w. 12½″ (32 cm.)
Collection of Yuasa Hachirō Memorial Museum

A unique ceremonial tsutsugaki textile made in the Izumo area was a
long sash for carrying an infant. Usually the child's maternal grandparents
prepared a ceremonial sash along with diapers and towels. Two similar
sashes are illustrated here. They are decorated with auspicious motifs. The
ends of the first sash carry small shōchikubai designs of pine, bamboo,
and plum. The second sash has more elaborate end designs: Treasure Ship
cape of invisibility, lucky mallet, flaming pearl, money bag, and scrolls
at one end and a little world of Mount Hōrai—pine, bamboo, crane, and
tortoise—at the other. The center section of the first sash is decorated with
a flower-diamond family crest. Two crests in the center of the second
sash probably identify the families of the bride and groom: one is *myōga*
(*Zingiber*, a type of ginger), a homonym of which means divine protection; the other is the familiar mokkō, melon. Customarily a sash was
saved for auspicious occasions; however, in the case of these sashes,
vertical faded lines, caused by folds, indicate they were frequently used.

40.   41.

42. Portion of a girl's kimono (p. 102)
Kaga (Ishikawa Prefecture), late 18th century
Hemp, hand spun, hand woven, plain weave, rice-paste resist, painted
 pigments, dip-dyed in indigo
Natural white, grey, moss green, red-brown, and pale yellow on indigo
 blue
Four-panel construction; 14″ panel
l. 35½″ (90 cm.); w. 59″ (150 cm.)
Honolulu Academy of Arts, purchase, 1937 (#4301)

A cotton or hemp kimono decorated with tsutsugaki designs and dip-
dyed in indigo is quite rare. This unusual example of hemp tsutsugaki is
the bottom portion of a girl's kimono that was probably worn at the
New Year or the November 15 Shichigosan (seven-five-three) Festival.
At Shichigosan girls three and seven years old dress in special kimono
and go with their parents to pray at the local shrine for a happy and safe
journey to adulthood. A kimono of this size was probably worn by a
seven year old. Against an indigo blue ground, a design of auspicious pine
trees and bamboo leaves spreads across the hem. Four small tortoises
happily swim in the water beneath the trees and, as a decorative conven-

tion, a large tortoise elevates himself and joins three energetic cranes flying in the sky. Subtle and subdued colors, delicate shading, and fine tsutsugaki lines are reminiscent of silk yūzen kimono technique.

43. *Nobori*   (p. 103)
Western Japan, Meiji period (1868–1912)
Hemp, hand spun, hand woven, plain weave, rice-paste resist, painted pigments
Black, brown, red, blue, yellow, moss green, and blue-grey on natural hemp color
Single-panel construction; 37″ panel
l. 285″ (752 cm.); w. 37″ (94 cm.)
Honolulu Academy of Arts, gift of Mrs. Norman Sterry, 1963 (#2.452)

This Boy's Day banner depicts typical, colorful warrior figures, a favorite masculine theme of this festival. Tsutsugaki banners are usually made in a two-step process. First, outlines of figures and other design elements are drawn in rice paste with a tsutsu onto cloth. Then, colorful pigments are painted directly onto the cloth, filling in the open sections of the design. The background is also painted in or parts may be left white. When the rice paste is washed off, the piece is completed. Dip-dyeing is not involved; the blue of this banner comes from painting with indigo pigment (*aibō*). The banner's warrior scene comes from the Heike-Genji wars. The central figure in the composition is Benkei, the monk-warrior retainer of Minamoto Yoshitsune (1159–89). Yoshitsune and Benkei were destroyed by the shogun, the elder brother of Yoshitsune, Minamoto Yoritomo (1148–99), in a struggle for power. Benkei's strength and bravery were legendary and he was a popular hero of literature and drama. In this scene, Benkei brandishes a lance from the back of a black steed. His head is covered by a monk's cap, rather than a samurai helmet, but he wears a warrior's armor. Although the design is decorative and conventional, the tsutsugaki craftsman's rendering shows the skill of an experienced hand. The relatively mellow, subdued hues and the delicate shading of colors set this banner apart from the more brilliant and opaque-colored Boy's Day banners that are usual.

44. *Maiwai*   (p. 85)
Boso Peninsula (Chiba Prefecture), Meiji period (1868–1912)
Cotton, hand woven, plain weave, rice-paste resist, stencil and cone drawing, painted pigments, dip-dyed in indigo
Natural white, rose, yellow, red-brown, light blue, grey, moss green, and black on indigo blue
Kimono construction, shortened with a tuck at the middle; 13″ panel
l. (hem to neck) 50″ (127 cm.); collar 2½″ (6 cm.); w. (sleeve to sleeve) 50″ (127 cm.)
Honolulu Academy of Arts, purchase, 1984 (#5243.1)

The maiwai was a special ceremonial outer kimono, or jacket, that fishermen of the Boso Peninsula (south of Tokyo) wore to inaugurate the New Year or to celebrate a rich catch. Early maiwai were made entirely by tsutsugaki technique; the design in this later example has been created by the simpler stencil method. Rice paste was applied through stencils and pigments were then brushed on. The faces were directly hand painted in red and black ink by an artist who specialized in painting faces. A tsutsu was used to add small dots above the hem and to cover the whole design prior to dip-dyeing in indigo. At the bottom of the kimono, three dancer-musicians celebrate a big catch by performing what is probably the Kashima Dance, an auspicious folk dance of the Kanto area that celebrates the religious world of Miroku (Maitreya). The central figure carries a large Shinto offering of paper in his right hand while he dances. A fan, in his left hand, has written on it in large red characters, "Great Catch" (*tairyō*). The figure on the right beats a drum, and the one on the left plays a flute. At the top of the kimono a large red family crest, mokkō, is superimposed over a crane in flight. The crane tows a small banner marked with a logo. This particular combination of crest and crane was common in later maiwai. A maiwai is worn over a kimono as a jacket and is not tied with a sash.

45. *Kazuki* or *Katsugi* (p. 86)
Shonai (Yamagata Prefecture), ca. 1750
Hemp, hand spun, hand woven, plain weave, rice-paste resist, stencil, cone drawing, dip-dyed in indigo, brushed ink
Natural white and light blue on blue-black
Kimono construction, without narrow front panels (*okumi*); $12\frac{1}{2}''$ panel
l. (hem to shoulder) 52" (132 cm.); collar 3" (8 cm.); w. (sleeve to sleeve) 48" (122 cm.)
Honolulu Academy of Arts, gift of Miss Frances Bieber, 1955 (#2036.1)

This lovely kazuki is made of fine-hemp material that is partially transparent. The neck has been lowered two and one-half inches below the shoulder line, forming a pocket that will conceal the head. It is made without the two narrow front panels that are a standard part of kimono construction. The dramatic black and blue wheel pattern at the top is balanced at the bottom by blue maple leaves and a flowing stream against a black ground. These designs were hand drawn by tsutsu. (The repeating flower patterns on the midsection and sleeves were made by stencil). The wheel pattern was inspired by the ox-drawn carts of Heian-period nobility. The wheel that kept turning without end was considered auspicious. The image of maple leaves and flowing water was popular in Japanese poetry long before the Momoyama period, when it became a favorite motif in decorative arts. Textile artisans in the Yamagata area produced many kazuki that juxtapose dramatic motifs, like the wheel and water-and-leaf designs of this garment, against a ground of small repeating patterns.

46. *Noren*   (p. 87)
Tsuruoka City (Yamagata Prefecture), Meiji period (1868–1912)
Hemp, hand spun, hand woven, plain weave, rice-paste resist, dip-dyed
   in indigo, brushed ink; hand woven, plain weave, indigo-dyed cotton
   loops
Natural white on black ground
Five-panel construction; 14″ panel
l. 67″ (169 cm.); w. 70″ (177 cm.)
Honolulu Academy of Arts, purchase, 1985 (#5337.1)

A fine example of a ceremonial noren. Probably brought as part of a trousseau and hung between rooms in the bride's new home. Coarse threads of hand-spun hemp rather loosely woven make a pleasant semi-transparent hanging. A large family crest in white of climbing wisteria (*nobori fuji*) spreads over three panels. Wisteria is one of the most graceful and intricate crest patterns, made famous by the prominent Fujiwara (wisteria field) political family in Heian times. Below and behind the eye-catching crest, bamboo trees, including a new shoot, sprout upward and outward from an ideal garden spot of rocks, grass, and bubbling stream. The simple, extremely linear design is strikingly beautiful and possesses an inner tension. The artist-craftsman contrasts living, realistic trunks and leaves of bamboo drawn of fine white tsutsu lines, with conventionally decorative rocks, water, and crest. The blue-black ground is probably achieved by brushing ink over indigo.

47. *Noren*   (p. 104)
Kaga (Ishikawa Prefecture), Meiji period (1868–1912)
Cotton, hand spun, hand woven, plain weave, rice-paste resist, painted
   pigments, dip-dyed in indigo
Natural white, grey, light blue, rose, and black on indigo blue
Three-panel construction; 13¼″ panel
l. 38½″ (98 cm.); w. 67″ (170 cm.)
Collection of James R. and Reiko M. Brandon, Honolulu

This elegant noren once hung in a home in the Kaga area, at the entry to a room or corridor. Fine white lines delineate four elegant cranes—two standing in the foreground among low pine shrubs and two approaching from a distance in the air. The well-balanced vertical design, with a large empty space above as background, is reminiscent of a hanging picture scroll. Ink lines drawn directly on the cloth skillfully delineate the crane's feathers. Faces, necks, and bodies have been delicately shaded in grey and blue in a manner that is both realistic and decorative. A touch of rose on the cranes' heads, eyes, and legs adds a graceful accent. A soft feminine beauty pervades this auspicious design. The craftsman who created this piece may have known silk yūzen dyeing, which flourished in the Kaga area, for the fastidious skill of the design is reminiscent of yūzen dyeing. The curtain was hung by two loops attached to the top corners. The three panels separate from the midpoint of the curtain, an unusually low position.

48. Hanging made from a jacket   (p. 88)
Place unknown, 17th century
Cotton, hand spun, hand woven, plain weave, rice-paste resist, painted
    with pigments, dip-dyed in indigo
Ochre, grey, and light brown on indigo blue
Irregular four-panel construction; 13″ panel
l. 46½″ (118 cm.); w. 48″ (122 cm.)
Honolulu Academy of Arts, purchase, 1937 (#4296)

This remarkable and rare piece was originally a short jacket, the six panels of which were resewn into a four-panel cloth. A horizontal seam, just above the tail of the horse in the center, shows where the collar of the jacket once was sewn. The slanting seam in the right panel probably shows the bottom of a sleeve, while another sleeve section, running horizontally, finishes the upper left of the cloth. Five wonderfully alert horses were painted directly on the jacket in pigments and then covered with rice paste, using a tsutsu, prior to dip-dyeing in indigo. The horses are shown realistically in varied poses and phases of action. The expressive faces, large eyes, and skillful, rhythmic composition suggest a painting prototype may have been used. Horses have been associated with warriors in Japan since prehistoric times, as baked clay haniwa horse figures (ca. A.D. 200–400) witness. The animal's vitality, strength, courage, and faithfulness were treasured by the samurai. In feudal times a prized horse was a valued offering to a Shinto shrine, where it would become a sacred mount for a deity. Painted horses (ema) are still presented to shrines as a less expensive, substitute gift. The jacket originally may have been worn by a servant of a samurai.

Notes

INTRODUCTION

1. Asa is a general term in Japanese for bast fibers, including hemp, ramie, linen, and others. The type of asa used for country tsutsugaki was almost always coarse hemp, while ramie was used for chayazome. Linen was not known in Japan until the Meiji period. See Okui Shirō, "Asa no kenkyū nōto" (Research notes on asa), *Senshoku arufā,* 41 (August 1984), p. 10.

2. Kamakura Yoshitarō, "Funanori fūzoku to yūsō na some" (Customs of fishermen and dyeing's grandeur), in Nakae Katsumi, ed., *Tsutsugakizome* (Tsutsugaki dyeing) (Tokyo: Tairyūsha, 1977), pp. 114–17.

3. Nippon Sen'i Kyōgikai, ed., *Nippon Sen'i Sangyōshi* (History of Japanese textile industry), 2 vols. (Tokyo: Nippon Sen'i Kyōgikai, 1958), vol. 2, pp. 17–18.

FUNCTION

1. Wakamori Tarō, *Hadashi no shomin* (Barefoot commoners) (Tokyo: Yūshindō, 1957), pp. 81–87.

2. Segawa Kiyoko, *Nihonjin no ishokujū* (Japanese clothing, food, and housing) (Tokyo: Kawade Shobō, 1964), pp. 126–38.

3. Oka Yoshishige, "Yogi," in Ishizuka Takatoshi, ed., *Izumo Oki no mingu* (Folk implements of Izumo and Oki) (Tokyo: Keiyūsha, 1971), p. 25.

4. Kitagawa Shūtei, *Ruijū kinsei fūzokushi* (Encyclopedia of Edo-period customs) (Tokyo: Bunchōsha, 1927), p. 570.

5. Kitamura Tetsurō, *Nippon fukushoku shōjiten* (Concise dictionary of Japanese costumes and accessories) (Tokyo: Genryūsha, 1979), p. 84.

6. "Tsutsumu tame no furoshiki," in Sanseidō, ed., *Furoshiki* (Tokyo: Sanseidō, 1984), p. 76.

7. Kitamura Tetsurō, *Yūzenzome* (Yūzen dyeing), in *Nippon no bijutsu* (Japanese art), no. 106 (Tokyo: Shibundō, 1975), p. 19.

8. Wakamori Tarō, *Hadashi no shomin,* pp. 178–81.

9. Yamanobe Tomoyuki, *Shomin no senshoku* (Textiles of commoners), in *Nihon no senshoku* (Japanese textiles), no. 9 (Tokyo: Chūō Kōronsha, 1983), pp. 76–79, and Nakatani Hisashi, "Tsutsugaki no

furusato Sanuki" (Sanuki, home of tsu-tsugaki), in Nakae Katsumi, ed., *Tsutsu-gakizome*, p. 104.

10. Kitamura Tetsurō, *Nippon fukushoku shōjiten*, p. 26.

11. Motoyama Keisen, *Seikatsu minzoku zusetsu* (Pictorial record of daily life) (Tokyo: Hakkō Shoten, 1943), p. 29.

12. Motoyama Keisen, *Seikatsu minzoku zusetsu*, p. 29.

13. Motoyama Keisen, *Seikatsu minzoku zusetsu*, p. 31.

MOTIFS

1. Iwasaki Haruko, *Nippon no ishō jiten* (Dictionary of Japanese design) (Tokyo: Iwasaki Bijutsusha, 1984), p. 38.

2. Kosugi Kazuo, *Nippon no mon'yō: kigen to rekishi* (Japanese design: origin and history) (Tokyo: Shakai Shisōsha, 1969), pp. 145–49, favors China, while Mori Yutaka thinks Persia, India, or Egypt is the source (Kitamura Tetsurō, *Nippon no mon'yō* [Japanese design] [Tokyo: Genryū-sha, 1983], p. 22).

3. Kosugi Kazuo, *Nippon no mon'yō*, pp. 123–25.

4. Morita Kimio, *Shishū* (Embroidery), in *Nippon no bijutsu* (Japanese art), no. 59 (Tokyo: Shibundō, 1971), pp. 19–21.

5. Iwasaki Haruko, *Nippon no ishō jiten*, pp. 38–39.

6. John W. Dower, *The Elements of Japanese Design* (Tokyo: Weatherhill, 1971), p. 68, and Nosaka Toshio, *Nippon kamon taikan* (Overview of Japanese family crests) (Tokyo: Shinjinbutsu Ōraisha, 1979), pp. 216–17.

7. Watanabe Soshū, *Tōyō zuan bunkashi no kenkyū* (Study of the cultural history of Oriental design) (Tokyo: Fuzanbō, 1951), pp. 69–89.

8. Watanabe Soshū, *Tōyō zuan bunkashi no kenkyū*, pp. 34–55.

9. Kawatake Toshio, ed., *Engeki hyakka daijiten* (Encyclopedia of theatre), vol. 3 (Tokyo: Heibonsha, 1960), p. 145.

10. John W. Dower, *The Elements of Japanese Design*, pp. 29 and 76. A forked radish is the symbol of the bodhisattva of fertility, Daishō Kankiten—Great Saintly Pleasure Deity—(Vinayakusha). See: Nosaka Toshio, *Nippon kamon taikan*, p. 264.

11. Shinshi Yoshimoto and Katō Hideyuki, *Nihon no kamon* (Japanese family crests) (Tokyo: Shokusandō, 1964), p. 231, and John W. Dower, *The Elements of Japanese Design*, pp. 3 and 4.

12. Nosaka Toshio, *Nippon kamon taikan*, p. 85.

TECHNIQUE

1. Yamanobe Tomoyuki, ed., *Some* (Dyeing), in *Nippon no bijutsu* (Japanese art), no. 7 (Tokyo: Shibundō, 1966), pp. 29–34.

2. Endō Yasuo, "Kenkōteki na shomin no some: tsutsugaki shōshi" (Healthy dyeing of the common people: short history of tsutsugaki), in Nakae Katsumi, ed., *Tsutsugakizome*, p. 137.

3. Yamanobe Tomoyuki, ed., *Some*, pp. 44–46.

4. Kitamura Tetsurō believes the area planned for the pattern was first covered with rice paste from a tsutsu, the ground was dyed, and the paste removed, leaving the design area white. Next, a tsutsu was used to draw with rice paste the outline of the umbrella within the design area and the open areas within the umbrella were painted with sumi and indigo. When the rice paste was removed the second time, the outline of the umbrella remained in white (*Yūzenzome*, pp. 49–53). Yamanobe Tomoyuki, in *Some*, pp. 55–59, briefly suggests the design was made by stencil.

5. Kosode is the classic term for a one-layer garment. Its cut is generally similar to the modern kimono. The term kosode was known in Heian times. From Muromachi through Edo times the kosode was the basic garment worn by both men and

women of all classes. Kosode, "small sleeve," means the wrist opening in the sleeve is small, not that the sleeve is short (kimono with trailing sleeves, *furisode*, are one type of kosode).

6. Kitamura Tetsurō, *Yūzenzome*, pp. 49–53.

7. Kamakura Yoshitarō, "Funanori fūzoku to yūsō na some," in Nakae Katsumi, ed., *Tsutsugakizome*, p. 111, and Kamakura Yoshitarō, "Ryūkyū bingata," *Senshoku to seikatsu* (Textiles and living), no. 9 (Summer 1975), p. 33.

8. Kitamura Tetsurō, *Yūzenzome*, p. 18.

9. Yūzen's unclear relationship to yūzen patterns is examined by Kitamura Tetsurō, *Yūzenzome*, pp. 21–26. We do not know when Yūzen was born or when he died. A book of kimono patterns, *Yosei hiinagata*, published in 1692, is signed "by the fanmaker Yūzen, living in front of Chion'in Temple [Kyoto]."

10. Hanaoka Shin'ichi, "Kaga tsutsugaki momen" (Cotton tsutsugaki textiles of Kaga), *Senshoku arufā*, no. 33 (December 1983), pp. 18–19.

11. Colorful bingata textiles may either be made by tsutsugaki or katazome technique. They have been produced in Okinawa at least since the eighteenth century and perhaps as early as the fifteenth century. In general bingata textiles were expensive and originally intended for the royal family or high members of the warrior class. Bingata wrapping cloths (*uchukui*), however, were commonly used at marriage ceremonies of samurai, including those in the middle and lower ranks, and bingata banners and curtains for theatres and funerals were made in tsutsugaki technique. Today, bingata ceremonial wrapping cloths as well as curtains are still produced. See: Watanaki Akira, "Tsutsugaki no bingata," in Nakae Katsumi, ed., *Tsutsugakizome*, pp. 190–99.

12. Gotō Shōichi, "Tsutsubikizome no yōzai" (Materials for dyeing tsutsugaki), in *Mingei tsutsugaki* (Folk tsutsugaki)

(Kyoto: Kyoto Shoin, 1969), pp. 1–6. Also see chart in Eisha Nakano and Barbara B. Stephan, *Japanese Stencil Dyeing: Paste-Resist Techniques* (Tokyo: Weatherhill, 1982), pp. 90–91.

13. This description of the Nagata family's working process is based on personal observation by the author, April 1984, and two published sources: Nagata Yasushi's own account in "Izumo iwai furoshiki no tsutsugaki gihō" (Tsutsugaki technique of Izumo ceremonial wrapping cloths), *Senshoku arufā*, no. 33 (December 1983), pp. 22–26, and Tsunoyama Yukihiro, *Fukusa furoshiki* (Kyoto: Miyai, 1970), pp. 44–52.

14. Chemical and physical functions of lime and bran in the paste are given in Eisha Nakano and Barbara B. Stephan, *Japanese Stencil Dyeing*, pp. 26–27.

15. See Eisha Nakano and Barbara B. Stephan, *Japanese Stencil Dyeing*, p. 69.

COTTON

1. Yanagida Kunio, "Momen izen no koto" (Life before cotton), *Yanagida Kunio-shū* (Collected works of Yanagida Kunio), vol. 14 (Tokyo: Chikuma Shobō, 1962), p. 9.

2. These textiles were probably made in Central Asia and brought to Japan via China. The woven structure of the fragments is similar to silk weaving practiced at the time (*tatenishiki*). (Nishimura Hyōbu, ed., *Orimono* [Weaving], in *Nippon no bijutsu* [Japanese art], no. 12 [Tokyo: Shibundō, 1967], pp. 83–85).

3. Cotton was first grown in Korea during the reign of Kyōbin (1351–74) and soon after it was being exported to Japan. Early in the sixteenth century, Chinese cotton largely replaced Korean cotton in the Japan market. For data on textile exports to Japan, see: Tsunoyama Yukihiro, "Momen no rekishi" (History of cotton), *Senshoku to seikatsu* (Textiles and living), no. 25 (Summer 1979), p. 21.

4. Noma Mitsutatsu, ed., *Nihon kōki* (Chronology of Japanese history), vol. 28 of *Tenritoshokan zenpon gyōsho* (Collection of the Tenri library) (Tokyo: Yagi Shoten, 1978), p. 55.

5. See Tsunoyama Yukihiro, "Momen no rekishi," p. 20.

6. A poem by the imperial court official Fujiwara Ieyoshi (1192–1264) describes the failure, "a foreigner who is not Japanese planted cotton seeds which did not grow" (*shikishimaya yamato ni wa aranu karabito no uenishi wata no tane wa taenishi*). Quoted in Nishimura Hyōbu, ed., *Orimono* (Weaving), p. 84.

7. Hibi Akira, "Momen hinshu no hensen" (Transition in cotton species), *Senshoku to seikatsu* (Textiles and living), no. 25 (Summer 1979), pp. 10–11.

8. See Tsunoyama Yukihiro, "Momen no rekishi," p. 21 for a discussion of the shrine document (*Daijōin jisha zōjiki*) and accounts of sixteenth-century cotton cultivation in *Journal of 1596–1614* (*Keichō kenbunshū*) and *Craft Documents* (*Kōgei shiryō*). Uemura Rokurō argues for an earlier date in his article "Tōrai momen orimono kō" (Study of introduced cotton weaving), *Senshoku to seikatsu* (Textiles and living), no. 25 (Summer 1979), p. 40. He infers from an account in *Records of the Suzuka Family* (*Suzukakeki*) (1394) of three servants receiving a quantity of cotton that cotton was cheap and therefore was produced locally at that time.

9. Morisue Yoshiaki et al., eds., *Seikatsushi* (History of daily life), in *Taikei nihonshi gyōsho* (History of Japan series), vol. 2 (Tokyo: Yamakawa Shuppansha, 1965), p. 200.

10. See Gotō Shōichi, "Nippon momen zufu" (Pictorial record of Japanese cotton), *Senshoku to seikatsu* (Textiles and living), no. 25 (Summer 1979), p. 58.

11. See illustration of a man spinning in Gotō Shōichi's rare collection, *Nihon senshokufu* (Pictorial records of Japanese textiles) (Tokyo: Tōhō, 1964), p. 65.

12. William B. Hauser, *Economic Institu-tional Change in Tokugawa Japan, Osaka and the Kinai Cotton Trade* (London: Cambridge University Press, 1974), p. 141.

13. William B. Hauser, *Economic Institutional Change,* p. 123.

14. Morisue Yoshiaki et al., eds., *Seikatsushi,* p. 273.

15. Segawa Kiyoko, *Nihonjin no ishokujū,* pp. 130–31.

16. See illustrations in Gotō Shōichi, *Nihon senshokufu,* pp. 13 and 64.

17. Two alternate characters have been used to write izari: one refers to the position of sitting in place and one means a cripple. There are several types of izari-bata: some have a wooden bench for the weaver, some have no bench, some have frames that are straight, some have slanted frames. It was also called a ground loom (*jibata*) if the weaver sat on the floor.

18. Shigematsu Seiji, "Nippon no teoriki: bunrui to chihōteki tokuchō" (Japanese hand looms: analysis and regional characteristics), *Senshoku arufā,* no. 49 (April 1985), p. 2.

Indigo

1. Uemura Rokurō, "Ai to ningen no seikatsu" (Indigo and human life), *Senshoku to seikatsu* (Textiles and living), no. 10 (Fall 1975), pp. 68–69.

2. Tsujimura Kiichi, "Injigo o fukumanai shimpi no yama ai" (Mysterious mountain indigo, not true indigo), *Senshoku arufā,* no. 49 (April 1985), pp. 63–64.

3. Gotō Shōichi, *Nippon senshokufu,* pp. 424–25.

4. For a useful English summary of indigo-dyeing methods see Monica Bethe, "Color: Dyes and Pigments," in *Kosode: 16th–19th Century Textiles from the Nomura Collection* (New York: Japan Society and Kodansha, 1984), pp. 73–75.

5. Yamazaki Seiju, "Man'yōshū no senshoku: mihanada" (Dyeing in the Man'yōshū: indigo blue), *Senshoku arufā,* no. 42 (September 1984), p. 50, and Maeda

Ujō, "Nippon kodai no ai" (Indigo in ancient Japan), *Senshoku to seikatsu* (Textiles and living), no. 10 (Fall 1975), p. 74.

6. Illustration in Gotō Shōichi, *Nippon senshokufu,* p. 250.

7. Illustration in Gotō Shōichi, *Nippon senshokufu,* p. 238.

8. Illustration in Gotō Shōichi, *Nippon senshokufu,* p. 252.

9. Morisue Yoshiaki, *Seikatsushi,* vol. 2, pp. 151–52.

10. Endō Motoo, *Nihon shokuninshi* (History of Japanese artisans) (Tokyo: Yūzankaku, 1967), p. 206.

11. Endō Motoo, *Nihon shokuninshi,* p. 213.

12. Endō Motoo, *Nihon shokuninshi,* pp. 201–3.

13. Endō Motoo, *Nihon shokuninshi,* pp. 207 and 208.

14. Ueda Toshio, *Awa ai minzokushi* (Folk history of Awa indigo) (Tokushima: Kyōiku Shuppan Sentā, 1983), p. 45.

15. Based on personal observation and interviews with Satō Akito, September 1985. A brief description is also given in the news sheet *Awa aizukuri* (Making Awa indigo), distributed by the Awaai Seisaku Gijutsu Hozonkai (Association for the preservation of the technique of making Awa indigo), 1984, 4 pages.

16. "Teitahō" (Hand paper testing), *Senshoku to seikatsu* (Textiles and living), no. 10 (Fall 1975), p. 21.

17. Makabe Jin, *Beni to ai* (Safflower and indigo) (Tokyo: Heibonsha, 1979), p. 24.

Bibliography

Bethe, Monica. "Color: Dyes and Pigments." In *Kosode: 16th–19th Century Textiles from the Nomura Collection*, ed. Naomi Noble Richard and Margot Paul, 58–76. New York: Japan Society and Kodansha, 1984.

Dower, John W. *The Elements of Japanese Design*. Tokyo: Weatherhill, 1971.

Endō, Motoo. *Nihon shokuninshi* (History of Japanese artisans). Tokyo: Yūzankaku, 1967.

Endō, Yasuo. "Kenkōteki na shomin no some: tsutsugaki shōshi" (Healthy dyeing of the common people: short history of tsutsugaki). In *Tsutsugakizome* (Tsutsugaki dyeing), ed. Nakae Katsumi. Tokyo: Tairyūsha, 1977.

Gotō Shōichi. *Nihon senshoku* (Pictorial records of Japanese textiles). Tokyo: Tōhō, 1964.

———. "Nippon momen zufu" (Pictorial record of Japanese cotton), *Senshoku to seikatsu* (Textiles and living), no. 25 (Summer 1979): 57–61.

———. "Tsutsubikizome no yōzai" (Materials for dyeing tsutsugaki). In *Mingei tsutsugaki* (Folk tsutsugaki). Kyoto: Kyoto Shoin, 1969.

Hanaoka, Shin'ichi. "Kaga tsutsugaki momen" (Cotton tsutsugaki textiles of Kaga), *Senshoku arufā*, no. 33 (December 1983): 13–21.

Hauser, William B. *Economic Institutional Change in Tokugawa Japan, Osaka and the Kinai Cotton Trade*. London: Cambridge University Press, 1974.

Hibi, Akira. "Momen hinshu no hensen" (Transition in cotton species), *Senshoku to seikatsu* (Textiles and living), no. 25 (Summer 1979): 9–14.

Iwasaki, Haruko. *Nippon no ishō jiten* (Dictionary of Japanese design). Tokyo: Iwasaki Bijutsusha, 1984.

Kamakura, Yoshitarō. "Funanori fūzoku to yūsō na some" (Customs of fishermen and dyeing's grandeur). In *Tsutsugakizome* (Tsutsugaki dyeing), ed. Nakae Katsumi. Tokyo: Tairyūsha, 1977.

———. "Ryūkyū bingata," *Senshoku to seikatsu* (Textiles and living), no. 9 (Summer 1975): 29–34.

Kawatake, Toshio, ed. *Engeki hyakka daijiten* (Encyclopedia of theatre). 6 vols. Tokyo: Heibonsha, 1960.

Kitagawa, Shūtei. *Ruijū kinsei fūzokushi* (Encyclopedia of Edo-period customs). Tokyo: Bunchōsha, 1927.

Kitamura, Tetsurō. *Nippon fukushoku shōjiten* (Concise dictionary of Japanese costumes and accessories). Tokyo: Genryūsha, 1979.

———, *Nippon no mon'yō* (Japanese design). Tokyo: Genryūsha, 1983.

———, ed. *Yūzenzome* (Yūzen dyeing). No. 106 of *Nippon no bijutsu* (Japanese art). Tokyo: Shibundō, 1975.

Kosugi, Kazuo. *Nippon no mon'yō: kigen to rekishi* (Japanese design: origin and history). Tokyo: Shakai Shisōsha, 1969.

Maeda, Ujō. "Nippon kodai no ai" (Indigo in ancient Japan), *Senshoku to seikatsu* (Textiles and living), no. 10 (Fall 1975): 72–75.

———. *Nippon kodai no shikisai to some* (Ancient Japanese colors and dyes). Tokyo: Kawade Shobō, 1975.

Makabe, Jin. *Beni to ai* (Safflower and indigo). Tokyo: Heibonsha, 1979.

Morisue, Yoshiaki et al., eds. *Seikatsushi* (History of daily life). Vol. 2 of *Taikei nihonshi gyōsho* (History of Japan series). 16 vols. Tokyo: Yamakawa Shuppansha, 1965.

Morita, Kimio. *Shishū* (Embroidery). No. 59 of *Nippon no bijutsu* (Japanese art). Tokyo: Shibundō, 1971.

Motoyama, Keisen. *Seikatsu minzoku zusetsu* (Pictorial record of daily life). Tokyo: Hakkō Shoten, 1943.

Nagata, Yasushi. "Izumo iwai furoshiki no tsutsugaki gihō" (Tsutsugaki technique of Izumo ceremonial wrapping cloths), *Senshoku arufā*, no. 33 (December 1983): 22–26.

Nakano, Eisha, and Barbara B. Stephan, *Japanese Stencil Dyeing: Paste-Resist Techniques*. Tokyo: Weatherhill, 1982.

Nakatani, Hisashi. "Tsutsugaki no furusato Sanuki" (Sanuki, home of tsutsugaki). In *Tsutsugakizome* (Tsutsugaki dyeing), ed. Nakae Katsumi. Tokyo: Tairyūsha, 1977.

Nippon Sen'i Kyōgikai, ed. *Nippon Sen'i Sangyōshi* (History of Japanese textile industry). 2 vols. Tokyo: Nippon Sen'i Kyōgikai, 1958.

Nishimura, Hyōbu, ed. *Orimono* (Weaving). No. 12 of *Nippon no bijutsu* (Japanese art). Tokyo: Shibundō, 1967.

Noma, Mitsutatsu, ed. *Nihon kōki* (Chronology of Japanese history). Vol. 28 of *Tenritoshokan zenpon gyōsho* (Collection of the Tenri library). Tokyo: Yagi Shoten, 1978.

Nosaka, Toshio. *Nippon kamon taikan* (Overview of Japanese family crests). Tokyo: Shinjinbutsu Ōraisha, 1979.

Oka, Yoshishige. "Yogi." In *Izumo Oki no mingu* (Folk implements of Izumo and Oki). ed. Ishizuka Takatoshi. Tokyo: Keiyūsha, 1971.

Okui, Shiro. "Asa no kenkyū nōto" (Research notes on asa), *Senshoku arufā*, no. 41 (August 1984): 10–25.

Segawa, Kiyoko. *Nihonjin no ishokujū* (Japanese clothing, food, and housing). Tokyo: Kawade Shobō, 1964.

Shigematsu, Seiji. "Nippon no teoriki: bunrui to chihōteki tokuchō" (Japanese hand looms: analysis and regional characteristics), *Senshoku arufā*, no. 49 (April 1985): 2–8.

Shinshi, Yoshimoto, and Katō Hideyuki. *Nihon no kamon* (Japanese family crests). Tokyo: Shokusandō, 1964.

"Teitahō" (Hand paper testing), *Senshoku to seikatsu* (Textiles and living), no. 10 (Fall 1975): 21–23.

Tsujimura, Kiichi. "Injigo o fukumanai shimpi no yama ai" (Mysterious mountain indigo, not true indigo), *Senshoku arufā*, no. 49 (April 1985): 63–65.

Tsunoyama, Yukihiro. *Fukusa furoshiki*. Kyoto: Miyai, 1970.

———. "Momen no rekishi" (History of cotton), *Senshoku to seikatsu* (Textiles and living), no. 25 (Summer 1979): 15–21.

"Tsutsumu tame no furoshiki." In *Furoshiki*, ed. Sanseidō, 76–77. Tokyo: Sanseidō, 1984.

Ueda, Toshio. *Awa ai minzokushi* (Folk history of Awa indigo). Tokushima: Kyōiku Shuppan Sentā, 1983.

Uemura, Rokurō. "Ai to ningen no seikatsu" (Indigo and human life), *Senshoku to seikatsu* (Textiles and living), no. 10 (Fall 1975): 68–71.

————. "Tōrai momen orimono kō" (Study of introduced cotton weaving), *Senshoku to Seikatsu* (Textiles and living), no. 25 (Summer 1979): 36–56.

Wakamori, Tarō. *Hadashi no shomin* (Barefoot commoners). Tokyo: Yūshindō, 1957.

Watanabe, Soshū. *Tōyō zuan bunkashi no kenkyū* (Study of the cultural history of Oriental design). Tokyo: Fuzanbō, 1951.

Watanaki, Akira. "Tsutsugaki no bingata." In *Tsutsugakizome* (Tsutsugaki dyeing), ed. Nakae Katsumi. Tokyo: Tairyūsha, 1977.

Yamanobe, Tomoyuki, ed. *Shomin no senshoku* (Textiles of commoners). No. 9 of *Nihon no senshoku* (Japanese textiles). Tokyo: Chūō Kōronsha, 1983.

————. ed. *Some* (Dyeing). No. 7 of *Nippon no bijutsu* (Japanese art). Tokyo: Shibundō, 1966.

Yamazaki, Seiju. "Man'yōshū no senshoku: mihanada" (Dyeing in the Man'yōshū: indigo blue), *Senshoku arufā*, no. 42 (September 1984): 48–52.

Yanagi, Sōetsu. *The Unknown Craftsman: A Japanese Insight into Beauty*. Tokyo: Kodansha International, 1972.

Yanagi, Sōri, ed. *Yanagi Sōetsu shūshū mingei taikan* (Yanagi Sōetsu folk crafts collection). 5 vols. Tokyo: Chikuma Shobō, 1981.

Yanagida, Kunio. *Momen izen no koto* (Life before cotton). Vol. 14 of *Yanagida Kunio-shū* (Collected works of Yanagida Kunio). Tokyo: Chikuma Shobō, 1962.

Acknowledgments

Numerous individuals and institutions contributed to the writing of this book and for their help I am deeply grateful. I would like especially to acknowledge the unfailing encouragement and support of George Ellis, director of the Honolulu Academy of Arts. With his extensive knowledge of the fabrics of Asia and Africa, he envisioned this book documenting the exhibition "Country Textiles of Japan: The Art of Tsutsugaki." I received unflagging cooperation from fellow staff members, especially Pam Jaasko of the textile department, Kathy Hoover, the director of the Academy shop, and Robert Ching, who photographed the exhibition pieces.

In Japan, scholars and institutions generously offered information and assistance: Tanaka Reiko and Sasaki Jun'ichi, curators at the Japanese Folk Crafts Museum; J. Edward Kidder, director of the Yuasa Hachirō Memorial Museum, and Saigō Yōko, curatorial assistant of the museum; Imanaga Seijirō, curator of decorative arts at Tokyo National Museum; Yotsumoto Takashi, professor of art at Tokyo Zōkei University; Katsumata Masako, curator of the Serizawa Keiji Museum; Morita Tadashi, Morita Folk Crafts; Tanaka Iwao, the Sanuki Folk Crafts Museum; Araki Kazuo, director of the Sanuki Folkway Museum; the Miki Indigo Library; Yonekawa Takahiro and Nonomura Toshio of the Industrial Research Center of Tokushima Prefecture; Satō Akito, owner of the Satō Indigo Farm; the Yumigahama Folk Crafts Museum; and the Izumo Folk Craft Museum. Tsutsugaki artisans Nagata Yasushi of Izumo City, Furushō Terumasa in Tokushima, and Ōkawahara Shizuo, Takamatsu City, and Fujimori Yōichi of the Fuji Paper Mills Cooperative in Tokushima shared their professional knowledge without reserve.

Important tsutsugaki pieces were graciously lent for the exhibition by the Yuasa Hachirō Memorial Museum in Tokyo, John and Barbara Stephan, Alex and Sandy Anderson, and George Ellis. Barbara Stephan gave invaluable writing advice and, with Alex Anderson, generously contributed photographs to illustrate the text. The old Japanese prints of dyeing are brought wonderfully alive in Dan Liu's sensitive line drawings.

I am grateful to the staff of John Weatherhill, Inc., for their encouragement and assistance. Candace Hand prepared the Glossary-Index.

My final bow goes to the multitude of unknown tsutsugaki craftsmen of the past two hundred years whose creations this exhibit celebrates.

Glossary-Index

Plate page numbers appear in italics at the end of each entry.

abalone, see *noshi* motif

abarenoshi: wild abalone strips, 90; see also *noshi* motif

aesthetics: of folk textiles, 3–5, 6, 7; of *tsutsugaki*, 8, 11, 33

ai, see indigo

aibō: precipitated indigo pigment, 33, 128

aidama: concentrated indigo pellets, 50

ai no hana: indigo fermentation bubbles, 51

Aizen Myōō: Buddhist guardian deity of dyers, 52

aizome momen: indigo-dyed cotton, 43

akane, see madder

Amami-Oshima: textiles, 6, 31–32

anchor motif, 16, 25

aobana: blue liquid extracted from *tsuyukusa* (a plant of the spiderwort family), used for marking patterns, 32

arrowroot (*kuzu*): a wild plant (*Pueraria lobata* Ohwi) whose fiber was used for weaving commoner's textiles, 6, 38

asa: a general term for bast fibers including hemp, ramie, and linen, and sometimes rough wild fibers as well, 3, 6, 19, 32, 38, 129, 133 n. 1

ashifuki: foot towel, 15, 16

awa ai: indigo grown in Awa, 47

baby-carrying sash, see *kooi*

baby towel, see *yuage*

back-strap loom, *see* looms: back-strap

bamboo motif, 21, 122 (Pl. 30); *76, 77, 80, 83, 87*

banana cloth, see *bashōfu*

banners, see *nobori*

bashōfu: Okinawan cloth woven of wild-banana (*ito bashō*) fibers, 6

bast fibers, see *asa*

bedding, see *futon*

bedding covers, see *futonji*

bengara: iron oxide, a red-brown inorganic pigment, 33

benibana, see safflower

bingata: Okinawan paste-resist dyeing technique using both tube-drawn and stenciled patterns, 8, 33, 135 n. 11

birth-related *tsutsugaki, see tsutsugaki:* birth-related

bokashi: color gradation or shading, 8

Boy's Day banners, see *nobori*

bridal *tsutsugaki, see tsutsugaki:* wedding-related

bureau covers, see *yutan*

characters, *see* ideographs

chayatsuji, see chayazome

chayazome (*chayatsuji*): summer kimono made of ramie and created by special *tsutsugaki* technique; worn by high-ranking samurai women, 3, 32, 33, 133 n. 1

cherry-blossom motif, *67*

chest covers, see *yutan*

chijimi: crepe, 6

childbirth-related textiles, see *tsutsugaki*: birth-related

China: and development of *tsutsugaki*, 8, 30, 44; influence on *tsutsugaki* motifs, 21–26; *see also* Plates; medicinal dye plants, 16, 43

Chinese characters: *see* ideographs

Chinese lion and peonies (*karajishi botan*) motif, 24–25; *60, 61*

chōji: an elongated clove pattern, one of the auspicious Collection of Treasures motifs, *78*

chrysanthemum motif, *67, 76, 77, 94*

cloud-pattern motif, *90*

Collection of Treasures (*takara zukushi*) motif: a decorative design made up of auspicious objects deriving from Chinese legend, *78, 97, 100–101*

color: application, 3, 7, 8, 29, 31, 32, 33, 35–37, 43–46; symbolism, 15–16, 31, 44, 126; *see also* dyes; pigments

colors: typical of *tsutsugaki*, 6, 15–16, 19, 33, 37, 43–44; *see also* Plates

compost, see *sukumo*

cotton: cultivation in Japan, 9, 38–40; dyeing, 34–37, 43; spinning and weaving, 39, 40–42

country *yūzen*, see *inaka yūzen*

crane and tortoise (*tsuru kame*) motif, 22; *59, 65, 68, 69, 98, 99, 102*

crane (*tsuru*) motif, 21–22; Fig. 3; *65, 75, 89, 92, 104*

crepe, 6

crests (*mon*): history and use as motifs, 12, 19, 20, 25–28; *see also* motifs; Plates; specific crests

Daruma: a Zen patriarch; as motif, 25; Fig. 15; *64*

diapers, see *mutsuki*

dip-dyeing, *see* indigo: dyeing process

dōfuku: a samurai's outer garment, 31

domestic objects: as motifs, 79

drum motif, *67, 85*

dyers/dye shops, 33, 34–37, 45–47, 53–54

dyes: application, 8, 32, 36, 37, 43–46; preparation, 44–45, 48–52; sources, 6, 15–16, 43–44; *see also* pigments

Edo (Tokugawa) period: dyeing techniques, 29, 32, 45, 46; dyemaking, 49, 50; dyers, 46, 47; motifs, 24, 27–28, 121, 124; textiles, 3–5, 6, 7, 11, 14–15, 17, 18–20, 32–33, 45; weaving, 39, 40–42

Egypt: influence on *tsutsugaki* motifs, 121

falcon-feather (*takanoha*) crest motif, 28; Fig. 16; *77, 84, 96*

family crests, see crests

fan motif: dancing, *69, 85*; open, *80, 95*

fermentation process, *see* indigo: dye bath

fisherman's jacket, see *maiwai*

flute motif, *67, 85*

folk crafts (*mingei*): preservation of, and *tsutsugaki*, 5

folk textiles: tradition of, in Japan, 4–10

foot print motif, 16

foot towels, 15, 16

fujiwa (wisteria ring) crest motif, *58*

fuji (wisteria) crest motif, *58, 87*

fundō: merchant's weights, one of the auspicious Collection of Treasures motifs, *78*

furisode: a long-sleeved kimono for young women, 134–35 n. 5

furoshiki: "bath spread," a wrapping and carrying cloth, 3, 11, 14–15; *81–84, 94–97*; traditional dyeing process, 34–37

futon: stuffed cotton bedding, 12–13

futonji: bedding cover, 4, 11; *see also* Plates

ganryō, see pigments

gojiru: a soybean-liquid dye binder, 32, 33, 35, 37, 120

gussets: in *yogi*, 13–14; *65–67*

haijiru: ash-lye water used to alkalize an indigo-dye bath, 51

hanabishi crest motif, *74*

of abalone, traditionally attached to a gift as an auspicious symbol, 25; *84, 90*

nyoihōju: "wish-come-true pearl," one of the auspicious Collection of Treasures motifs, *78, 90, 97*

oak crest motif, *67*

ocean waves motif, *69, 77, 80*

ōdo: iron hydroxide, an inorganic yellow or ochre pigment, 33

Ōkawahara Shizuo: a contemporary *tsutsugaki* and stencil-dye artisan, 53–54

Okinawa (Ryukyu Islands): dyemaking, 45; textiles, 6, 8, 31, 33, 135 n. 11

omodaka (water plantain) crest motif, *75*

omote kon'ya: "front dye shop," specialized in dyeing fabrics, 46

oshidori (mandarin duck) motif, *83*

paper mulberry: a tree (*Broussonetia papyrifera* Vent.) yielding a coarse fiber used in weaving, 38

paste-resist dyeing, 3, 8, 29–32; see also *katazome; yūzen*

paulownia and phoenix (*kiri hōō*) motif, 23–24; *62, 66, 70, 71*

paulownia motif, 23–24; *76*

pearl motif, *see* treasure-pearl motif

peony motif, *76, 77*

Persia: influence on *tsutsugaki* motifs, 22

persimmon juice: used to strengthen *tsutsugaki* paper cones, 29

phoenix (*hōō*) motif, 24; Fig. 11; *81; see also* paulownia and phoenix motif

pigments (*ganryō*), 8, 17, 32, 33–34, 37, 105, 111, 123, 129

pine, bamboo, plum motif, see *shōchikubai* motif

pine motif, 21; *67, 76, 77, 96, 102, 104*

plants: as dye source, 6, 16, 43–44, 126; as fiber source, 6, 38; see also *asa;* indigo

plum motif, 21; *64, 74, 76, 79, 80, 82*

ramie (*Urtica dioica* L.): a fine bast fiber, used to weave delicate fabrics, 3, 6, 32, 133 n. 1; see also *asa*

resist dyeing, *see* paste-resist dyeing

rice paste: as resist agent, 3, 29, 30, 32, 35, 135 n. 14

rōkechi: classic term for wax-resist dyeing, 29

rokuro: a hand-cranked cotton gin, 40; Fig. 27

Ryukyu Islands, *see* Okinawa

safflower (*benibana*): a thistle (*Carthamus tinctorius* L.) whose flowers produce a pink or red natural dye, 15–16, 126

sakiori: "tear and weave," a recyled weaving made of torn strips of used textiles, 6

samurai class: influence on *tsutsugaki* motifs, 107, 113, 115, 117, 131; textiles of, 3, 17, 32, 38

Satō family: prominent indigo growers in Tokushima Prefecture, 47–50

sekiō, see *kiō*

sekkai: lime, used to alkalize an indigo dye bath, 51

Seven Lucky Gods (*shichi fukujin*) motif, 118

sha (gauze), 32

shibori (*kōkechi*): resist dyeing achieved by tying, binding, sewing, or folding cloth prior to dyeing, 29, 32, 114

Shibuzawa Keizō: financier and folk-craft patron, 5

shichi fukujin (Seven Lucky Gods) motif, 118

shikibuton: under bedding, 79

Shikoku Island: *tsutsugaki* tradition, 7, 47, 53–54; *63, 64, 73, 79, 94*

shikunshi: the "four princes" of pictorial art: chrysanthemum, plum, bamboo, and orchid, 122

Shimane Prefecture, *tsutsugaki* tradition of, *see* Izumo

shina, see Japanese linden

Shingata komonchō, see New Style Pattern Book, The

shinshi: split bamboo stretchers used to hold cloth taut for drying and sometimes dyeing, 34, 35, 36, 37

shippō: Seven Treasures in lozenge shape, one of the auspicious Collection of Treasures motifs, *78*

shōaizome: "true indigo dyeing," a fermented-indigo dye process, 45

shōchikubai (pine, bamboo, plum) motif: an auspicious design especially felicitous for

wedding decorations and gifts, 21; Fig.
9; *57–59, 68, 69, 82, 93, 95, 100–101*
shrimp motif, 16, 25; Fig. 14
shu: mercuric sulfide, a red inorganic pigment, 33
snow motif, *77, 83*
sotetsu (cycad palm) motif, *73*
soybean liquid: a dye binder, 32, 33, 35, 37,
120
standing-tree motif, 106
stencil dyeing, see *katazome*
suehiro (open fan) motif, *80, 83*
sukumo: compost of fermented indigo leaves,
used to make an indigo dye bath, 45, 47–
51
sumi: ink made of pine lampblack, used as
a pigment, 33, 37, 120, 121
sword crest motif, *63, 66*

tabane noshi motif: joined abalone strips,
84; see also *noshi* motif
tachibana (orange flower and leaves) motif,
78
tachiki mon'yō (standing tree) motif, 106
tade ai (*Polygonum tinctorium* Lour.): the
chief type of indigo plant cultivated in
Japan, 44
takahata, see looms: high
takanoha, see falcon-feather crest motif
takarabune, see Treasure Ship
takarakagi: "treasure key," one of the auspicious Collection of Treasures motifs,
78
takara zukushi, see Collection of Treasures
motif
tangara, see mangrove
tatewaku motif: undulating vertical lines enclosing motifs, 77
tea-ceremony utensils: as motif, 25; *64, 79*
Tenjukoku shūchō, see Heavenly Embroidery
Tokugawa period, see Edo period
torikae momen: "bartered cotton," the custom of obtaining ginned cotton in ex-
change for hemp cloth, 40
tortoise motif, 22–23; *59, 63, 68, 69, 77, 80*
treasure-pearl motif, *78, 90, 97*
Treasure Ship (*takarabune*): a mythical ship
bearing auspicious objects, 118, 127; *see
also* Collection of Treasures motif

tsuru, see crane motif
tsurugi katabami: sword and wood-sorrel
crest motif, *63, 66*
tsuru kame, see crane and tortoise motif
tsuta (ivy) crest motif, *64*
tsutsu: a cone-shaped tube made of paper
and treated with persimmon juice, used
for drawing on fabric in paste-resist technique, 3, 29, 30, 35
tsutsugaki: aesthetics, 8, 11, 20, 33; birth-
related, 15–16; *98–101;* Chinese influence, 8, 21–26, 30, 44; contemporary
craftsmen, 9–10, 34–37, 53–54; distinc-
tiveness, 8, 32, 34; history, 8–9, 30–34;
rural tradition, 4, 5–7, 25, 33, 105, 118–
19; urban textiles, 4; wedding-related,
11–15; see also *chayazome; yūzen*
tsutsugaki momen: hand-drawn rice-paste resist cotton fabric, 7, 39

uchide no kozuchi: mallet of good fortune,
one of the auspicious Collection of
Treasures motifs, *78*

warrior motif, 17; *103*
wata uchiya: an artisan who fluffed cotton
with a special bow (*wata uchiyumi*), 41
wata uchiyumi: "cotton-striking bow," a
bow strung with a taut cord used to
fluff cotton, 40–41
waterfall motif, *61*
wax-resist dyeing, see *rōkechi*
weaving, 6–7, 9, 39, 40, 41–42
wedding-related *tsutsugaki,* see *tsutsugaki:*
wedding-related
wheel motif, *86*
white indigo, *see* indican
wild abalone, see *abarenoshi*
wild-banana cloth, see *bashōfu*
wisteria: fiber of the wild wisteria (*Wistaria
brachybotrys* Sieb. et Zucc.) used in weaving, 38; crest motif, *58, 87*
wood-sorrel crest motif, *63, 66*
wrapping cloth, see *furoshiki*

yama ai: "mountain indigo," a wild plant
(*Mercurialis leiocarpa* Sieb. et Zucc.) which
produces an impermanent blue, 43–44;
see also indigo

Yanagida Kunio: the father of modern folklore studies in Japan, 5, 38

Yanagi Sōetsu: leader and founder of the folk-craft movement in Japan, originator of the Folk Craft Museum, 5, 7, 9

yogi: "night wear," stuffed bed cover in kimono shape, 4, 11, 12, 13, 33, 53; *57, 58, 65–67*

yōkō: juice of the cochineal insect, a red-blue organic pigment, 33

yono: bedding made of four panels of fabric, 13

yuage: baby towel, 4, 15–16; *98*

yukiwa: "snow flake and circle" pattern, 31

yutan: bureau, chest cover, 4, 11, 14, 33; *81, 92, 93*

yūzen: popular paste-resist dye technique on silk developed in Kyoto in the seventeenth century, 3, 107, 111; history, 8, 32, 33; technique, 32, 128, 130; see also *tsutsugaki*

Yūzen (Yūzensai): Kyoto fan painter of the seventeenth century whose painting style influenced kimono dye patterns, 32, 135 n. 9

The "weathermark" identifies this book as a production of John Weatherhill, Inc., publishers of fine books on Asia and the Pacific. Supervising editor: Michael Ashby. Book design and typography: Miriam Yamaguchi. Production supervision: Mitsuo Okado. Layout of illustrations: Miriam Yamaguchi. Composition of text: Planet Press, Tokyo. Printing: Kyodo Printing Co., Tokyo. Binding: Makoto Binderies, Tokyo. The typeface used is Monotype Bembo.